Magellan Moon

Magellan Moon

A Travel Memoir

Roger Lee Kenvin

Verna Rudd Kenvin

July Blue Press

Published by July Blue Press
jlybl@earthlink.net

Copyright 2002 by Roger Lee Kenvin and Verna Rudd Kenvin

First printing

Printed in the United States of America by Odyssey Press Inc., Dover, New Hampshire

Library of Congress Control Number: 2001119467

ISBN 0-9656635-7-4

For Lois, Janet Ann, and Marion

who gave us a homecoming welcome

better than all the dancing beauties of Bali,

Hawaii, and Bora Bora put together

The ship in port is a tamed being, subject only to its crew's ministrations. But when it sails it trumpets out, in a deep harbor voice to quickening hearts that listen and never forget, promises of mystery, adventure, and the fulfillment of dreams.

Then it vanishes, as it came, a luminous wonder of the sea.

Roger Lee Kenvin

CONTENTS

PHOTOGRAPHS

Cover—Mount Vesuvius and the Bay of Naples.

Back Cover—(clockwise from top left) School-children in Nara, Japan; Balinese girl in Amlapur; Rudd in crowd at Capri; QE2 in Hong Kong harbor; Man on Camel in Giza, Egypt.

Royal Palace at Amlapur, Bali—after page 82.

Kasuga Taisha Shrine, Nara, Japan— after page 98.

Flower Market, Singapore—after page 124.

Gold Souk, Dubai, U.A.E.—after page 144.

Cours Mirabeau, Aix-en-Provence—after page 190.

Authors—after page 217.

All photographs by the authors

PREFACE

Before you read this book a few words are in order. On September 11, 2001, Rudd and I were on the Southwest Chief Amtrak train between Los Angeles and Chicago. We were heading for New Hampshire. I had just finished proofreading the manuscript of this book on the train and had already sent ahead a letter to Odyssey Press in New Hampshire asking for a price quote on it.

This was to be the seventh book which Odyssey would print for July Blue Press. Douglas Stone, Vice-President of Odyssey, had sent me quotes on all our books in the past. But this time there was to be no reply from him. Douglas was on American Airlines Flight 11 when it was hijacked and deliberately crashed into the World Trade Towers in New York.

My first impulse was to cancel the book entirely. I felt hurt, angry, confused, depressed, as did many others. Suddenly, the world which most of us had embraced so optimistically was filled with evil and horror. Innocent people like Douglas had been sacrificed cruelly by demonic terrorists. The book now seemed completely irrelevant and frivolous, my tone too satirical and light-hearted.

But when I talked with friends at Odyssey they were doing their best to continue with the work, as Douglas would have wanted them to. So it seemed to Rudd and me that we should too.

I have left the book as I finished it on September 11th. The final chapter describes the excitement at arriving back in New York harbor on April 20th. The World Trade Towers were there then, although it would be the last time we would ever see them.

But I have a long memory of my native New York. I can remember a time when there was an elegant Hotel Astor at Times Square, an Empire Theatre with a long-running *Life with Father,* a Metropolitan Opera House at Broadway and 39th Street, an Ebbets Field in Brooklyn, a Ritz-Carlton Hotel on Madison Avenue, a Wanamaker's Department Store down around 12th Street somewhere, and a magnificent 1939 New York World's Fair in Flushing Meadows.

I remember the thrill of meeting Paul Robeson backstage at the Shubert Theatre and chatting with the enchanting Margaret Sullavan after *The Voice of the Turtle* and being treated to dinner at Toffenetti's by my parents before I went into the U.S. Navy in World War II. Memories do not fade when they are turned into words. That is why books exist.

So the World Trade Towers are here, as I described them, tall and proud—"the twin exclamation points of New York" and the good work of Douglas Stone and Odyssey Press informs this work throughout as it has in the past and as it is meant to do now.

Roger Lee Kenvin

BREAKING NEWS FROM THE SOUTH CHINA SEA

March 8, 2001: An angry crowd gathers on the hard cement pier of the port city Vung Tau in Viet Nam. At any time it numbers between 300 and 400 people from countries all over the world, anxious to get back to the huge ocean liner at anchor in the South China Sea about forty minutes away.

But the sea is too rough and the risk of damage to passengers and the tenders that transport them too great. So the waiting game goes on.

Hours pass. The hot sun sets, a full moon rises. The heat of the day turns to the chill of the night air. People huddle closer, fearful of mosquitoes and malaria.

New buses pull up now, discharging people returning from a day in Saigon. One bus brings in a whole orchestra with opera singers scheduled to present a concert on board ship this evening. The pier is festive now with the long shadows of cellos, violins, oboes, drums, propped up alongside desolate, dejected musicians who can see they are going nowhere.

People no longer bother to queue up waiting for a tender. They form an amorphous mass, pointed toward the water. Desperation rides on foreheads. Territorial space and a pushing, forward movement motivate them now. Some people, sitting in white plastic molded chairs, clasp the chairs to their bottoms and inch along, squeezing their way through, like lemmings to the sea.

Up above, the moon smiles down at this silly charade of human impatience.

What time is the next boat to the QE2?

TWO IF BY SEA

"Two drifters, off to see the world.
There's such a lot of world to see."

Johnny Mercer

There must have been an errant moon that night in October 2000—perhaps one of those gorgeous, orange autumn moons that beguiles sailors, lunatics, werewolves, and whoever else is abroad. That included my wife, Rudd, and me.

As I remember it, we had just returned from a voyage on the *Seabourn Sun* originating in Canada and finishing in Fort Lauderdale in August, 2000. Back in our California home, we received in the mail one day a notice from *Travltips*, a freighter travel publication, advertising a P & O voyage around the world on the *Aurora* for about $11,000 each.

This can't be true, we thought. We were right. It wasn't. Rudd checked with *Travltips*, P & O, and with our travel agent, Janet Morton, at the Santa Barbara Travel Agency. The real price was more like $20,000 a person. For that, Janet thought she could get us a better deal on the QE2, since we had been on that ship many times before.

With Janet working on it, Rudd became more enthusiastic, saying that it had always been a lifetime dream of hers to sail around the world. We had already circled the globe by air in 1965-66 when we lived in India with our two children for the academic year and we had traveled extensively both going to and leaving India. But this trip would be special, on a luxury liner with a maximum potential for enjoyment.

We began by applying for an inside cabin, which, through Janet's special expertise and magic, soon became an outside cabin in the choice midships "E" area on Deck Four, Stateroom 4127. Rudd and I now began to prepare in earnest.

There would be our wardrobes to consider. The Cunard line is the dressiest of the lot and there were to be a staggering forty-four formal evenings as well as many gala balls during the voyage. Since the ship would be our home for three months, we wanted to travel as lightly as possible, but still have some variety in our clothes.

For evenings, Rudd took two long black skirts of slightly different fabrics and styles and eight different tops to wear with them, plus her beautiful lavender Benares sari from India to wear to the Raj Ball on board.

I took my tuxedo, plus a white dinner jacket, five different evening bow ties, three cummerbunds, and one evening vest in blue, plus three formal shirts. I considered taking my full Macdonald kilt, which looks nice as evening wear, but decided against it because of its heavy weight. (There were at least two men on the voyage who wore the kilt on formal occasions.)

One thing was certain about my wardrobe on this voyage. There would be no bluejeans or denim in any form. The English do not like denim and you see it usually only on Americans on Cunard ships or on young people from formerly Communist countries or others in permanent rebellion against good taste. Also, no cowboy boots, which I regularly wear in California. I also resolved to eat food like the British, fork held defensively, tines down, in the left hand, knife in the right, little stabs, dainty parries and thrusts, cutting up everything finely, throwing out a "yes, please," "thank you," or "lovely" more or less at regular intervals to anyone serving me at the table.

It can be both a problem and a blessing to sail on the QE2. You enter Great Britain the moment you board. I like it, of course, but others might not.

Here is a complete rundown of the wardrobe that I took with me. I think it is important to make a list so that you can travel as lightly as possible. I decided that the clothes I would wear boarding the ship would include my wool baseball cap, a black windbreaker, black corduroy pants, a short-sleeved shirt, and Reebok sneakers.

Roger's Wardrobe for the World Cruise

1. Tuxedo
2. White dinner jacket
3. Navy blue Alexander Shields suit
4. Tan gaberdine suit
5. White Brooks Brothers pants
6. Black loafers
7. Brown loafers
8. Blue Bermuda shorts
9. Burberry rain coat with lining
10. Navy blue Tilley hat
11. Navy blue Tilley pants
12. Navy blue long-sleeved wool sweater
13. Black turtleneck sweater
14. Navy blue sleeveless sweater
15. Three white dress shirts
16. Three white evening shirts
17. One green-and-blue striped dress shirt
18. One blue dress shirt
19. One tan dress shirt

20. One burgundy dress shirt
21. One long-sleeved Macdonald Pendleton wool shirt
22. One green Black Watch long-sleeved sport shirt
23. Four short sleeve sport shirts
24. Five nylon travel briefs
25. Four undershirts
26. Three knee-high dark wool socks
27. Three white knee-high socks
28. One lightweight Pierre Cardin bathrobe
29. Three pairs of sleeping boxer shorts
30. Flippers for bathroom or pool
32. Four belts, white, black, brown, tan
33. Assortment of bow ties
34. Twelve selected neckties
35. Cummerbunds (3) and evening vest

Rudd and I each have a brown American Tourister canvas suitcase with wheels and rising handle for easy management. In addition, I carried a small black briefcase for important papers and toilet articles. We also took a duffel bag on wheels and a Mac laptop with us on this trip, disguised in a Maupintour travel bag. Also, inside one of the suitcases we carried a deflated green soft canvas bag for the gifts we knew we would want to bring back for our grandchildren.

Both of us gave careful thought to our wardrobes. After all, we would be gone for three months, visiting varied climates from tropical to cool, quite different from the eternal June of southern California.

The itinerary looked like this:

Jan 19	Departure from Los Angeles
Jan 23, 24	Honolulu, Hawaii
Jan 28	Pago Pago, Samoa

Jan 31	Lautoka, Fiji
February 3,4	Auckland, New Zealand
Feb 7,8,9	Sydney, Australia
Feb 11	Hobart, Tasmania
Feb 12, 13	Melbourne, Australia
Feb 15	Adelaide, Australia
Feb 18	Fremantle, Australia
Feb 21, 22	Padang Bay, Bali, Indonesia
Feb 25	Manila, Philippines
March 1	Kobe, Japan
March 4,5,6	Hong Kong, China
March 8,9	Vung Tau (Ho Chi Minh City), Vietnam
March 11,12	Laem Chabang (Bangkok), Thailand
March 14,15	Singapore
March 17	Phuket, Thailand
March 20	Columbo, Sri Lanka
March 22	Mumbai (Bombay), India
March 25, 26	Dubai, United Arab Emirates
March 27	Muscat, Oman
April 1	Aqaba, Jordan
April 2	Safaga, Egypt
April 3,4	Port Suez (Cairo), Egypt
April 6,7	Naples, Italy
April 9, 10	Marseille, France
April 12	Lisbon, Portugal
April 14	Southampton, England
April 20	New York, U.S.A.

Some of these ports we had been to before. Others, like the Red Sea ports, would be new to us. We also had friends in Melbourne, Hong Kong, Southampton, and New York we knew we would want to see on this voyage.

Another point should be made here at the outset, and that has to do with a philosophy of travel. Why do we do it? If you don't explain your purpose, others gladly impose their own thinking on your travels, revealing only their own motivations, not yours. Both my wife and I use the *Queen Elizabeth 2* as transportation, the way others use airplanes and cars—to get from one place to another. We have to have definite destinations in mind, usually places we've not been to before.

The shore excursions are a major consideration. We avoid ships that zap around from one resort to another, usually in the Caribbean on the sun-sex-gambling-shopping circuit. That is not for us, nor is the kind of ship that features verandahs, highly-organized social activities, and a frenetic nightlife of any sort. The *Queen Elizabeth 2* is a ship, steady and seaworthy, with an experienced, considerate staff and crew, and a loyal clientele in a British ambience. Obviously, we like it that way, which is why we have traveled on Cunard ships since 1949 (in my wife's case) and 1953 (in my case).

Travel to us is a valuable part of the educational process, so we expect a lot from our land travel when we arrive in port. Cunard does an excellent job of providing land excursions, and, of course, one is free to sightsee completely on one's own. On this trip, for instance, we had been to Sydney before, so we used the three days there for our own purposes, going to the opera, shopping, and exploring. Again,we also left open Hong Kong, Southampton, and Melbourne, so that we could follow our own plans there.

Statistics: Putting the cart before the horse, here is what the whole trip cost us. Cunard adds the gratuities into the total bill, but one can give extra tips, as we generally do.

Cabin 4127 on *Queen Elizabeth 2*	$42,000
Land tours	4,000
Insurance	2,700

Tips on land tours	300
Shipboard extra tips to waiters, room steward	340
Gifts (mostly for grandchildren)	950
Miscellaneous (toiletries, bar bill, cleaning, photos on board ship, etc.)	600

$50,890

This is what it cost for the two of us. For a larger stateroom or a more extravagant lifestyle, figure on a higher amount. It could also be done less expensively. Remember, too, that my wife and I do not own a Mercedes Benz and we live in a townhouse. Travel, education, books are always top priorities for us.

After all the details were finalized and I knew we would be leaving on the voyage, I began thinking about Ferdinand Magellan and his attempt to circumnavigate the globe in 1519. He sailed under the auspices of King Charles V of Spain, putting to sea on September 20, 1519, with five ships of which the *Trinidad* was the flagship. Only one of the ships, the *Vittoria*, under command of Juan Sebastiano del Cano, completed the voyage and returned to Spain. The other ships were wrecked in storms and one was captured by pirates. Only eighteen of the original sailors ever made it back to Spain.

Ferdinand Magellan himself, that enterprising Portuguese who changed his citizenship to sail for Spain, never came home. Having endured a mutiny of his crew and rough seas, he was killed by natives in Mactan, the Philippines. The only memorial he had was having the Straits of Magellan between Patagonia and Tierra del Fuego named after him, his only satisfaction, reaching the Pacific Ocean.

I knew Magellan and his men had sailed from Seville on August 10, 1519 and then waited at the mouth of the Guadalquivir river until they braved the sea on September 20, and I wondered if there had been some strange, magnetic pull in the moon on those dates egging them on in their daring endeavor, something I called "a Magellan Moon."

Centuries later, had Rudd, I, and others who booked round-the-world cruises, been afflicted with the same kind of Magellan madness—an irresistible impulse to circumnavigate the globe by ship, raft, canoe, kayak, or sailboat? Airplanes don't count. Speed is not Magellan's way. Exploration only by ship is what matters.

Beware of the moon's beams on any August 10th or September 20th. It could be hazardous. You may just feel an uncontrollable desire to depart from the nearest port for exotic, distant lands.

Need I add—Take special care in the Philippines?

SLOW DISSOLVE AND FADE OUT

"All that sunshine can't be good for the brain."

Gloria Swanson

We have lived since 1995 in a townhouse in Arcadia, a residential area in the northeast corner of Los Angeles, near Pasadena, the metropolis of the San Gabriel Valley.

Arcadia is known primarily for its beautiful race track, Santa Anita, which is in walking distance from our house and to which we go perhaps once or twice a year with our daughters and grandsons or out-of-town visitors. The racetrack was built in the late 1920s by movie people like Lewis B. Mayer and Harold Lloyd. It has the dramatic backdrop of the San Gabriel Mountains and is itself beautifully landscaped and maintained. It has appeared in countless motion pictures, and when one visits it early in the morning at Clockers Corner one can glimpse celebrities like Jack Klugman, Tim Conway, or Burt Bacharach chatting with trainers or the colorfully dressed jockeys.

The other big attraction in Arcadia is the Los Angeles Arboretum with its graceful large trees, exotic plants, fountains, and resident peacocks. It, too, has been used as a backdrop in many films.

Like neighboring San Marino, Arcadia's population is about one-third Asian, largely Chinese, which means that our high school has some of the brightest, most hardworking students in Los Angeles and that we have some of the best restaurants. I understand that visitors from China often get off the plane at Los Angeles International Airport and head directly for the fine restaurants in and around Monterey Park, just to the south of Arcadia.

At any time in the Arcadia Public Library, about 90% of the people using it are of Asian background. This is also true of the post office, where long lines of people, largely Asian, send complicated gift packages to exotic destinations. For us, this makes for a very dynamic, always fascinating hometown.

Other parts of Los Angeles have their particular ethnic flavors, too. Neighborhoods seem constantly in a state of flux. The flats of Hollywood, for instance, have become increasingly Hispanic and the last time I was at the Grand Central Market on Broadway in downtown Los Angeles, it had the aura of a similar market in Tijuana, Mexico or Acapulco—colorful, animated, noisy.

Public television in Los Angeles has a popular program called *California's Gold,* hosted by likable Huell Howser, which explores many of the diverse regions and people of California. This series is also available on videotapes and is a perfect introduction to the Los Angeles and California I am trying to explain here.

People who enjoy a dynamic culture flourishing in a giant oasis in the middle of an enormous desert always enjoy Los Angeles. Within an hour or two from downtown L.A. one can go up to the Santa Monica or San Gabriel mountains for hiking, or to the San Bernardino mountains in the winter months for skiing, ice skating, or sledding. Boating people have the options of the celebrated small lakes, Arrowhead and Big Bear, or the marinas at Newport Beach or Marina del Ray.

There is also a golf, sun, and tennis paradise in Palm Springs; charming towns on the blue Pacific Ocean, La Jolla, San Clemente, Laguna Beach; long stretches of sandy white beach at Santa Monica,

Malibu, Trancas; posh residential houses in Bel Air and Beverly Hills; Bohemian hangouts in Silver Lake and West Hollywood; hidden delights like Beachwood Canyon leading up to the Hollywood Sign and reservoir; Watts for its famous towers; El Segundo for its old-time movie theatre; Long Beach for its Aquarium and *Queen Mary*; and countless other places—La Cienega Boulevard, for instance, for its great restaurants, including an English tea-room, Paddington's; East Los Angeles, Boyle Heights, Lincoln Park for their history and edginess; Exposition Park for its splendid Coliseum and its University of Southern California; Pasadena for its Rose Bowl and trendy Old Town area; Westwood for U.C.L.A. and its university town atmosphere (if you can find a parking place).

The one Los Angeles place that invariably disappoints visitors is Hollywood. I feel sure this is the result of a long-standing mistaken notion: People think that all the movie studios are located in one place and that Hollywood is like a small town in which one can walk around. The truth is that all of the studios are not and never have been in Hollywood. MGM, the studio of Clark Gable, Greta Garbo, Jean Harlow, Hepburn and Tracy, Judy Garland and Mickey Rooney has always been in Culver City, quite far from Hollywood. It is now the Sony Studios.

Warner Brothers is in Burbank, over the mountains from Hollywood, near Studio City and Universal City, where Universal Studios is located. Warners was the studio of Bette Davis, Errol Flynn, Humphrey Bogart, and James Cagney, among others.

Twentieth-Century-Fox, the studio of Shirley Temple, Alice Faye, Don Ameche, Tyrone Power, and Sonja Henie is out on Olympic Boulevard, again at a distance from Hollywood.

This leaves just a handful of film studios in Hollywood itself—Paramount, the old RKO (which became Desilu), the original Charlie Chaplin studio. What one sees along Hollywood Boulevard is a slew of souvenir shops selling T-shirts and videos, a lot of cheap, flashy places, only a few genuine gems—the Chinese Theatre, the Pantages Theatre, the Egyptian, the Hollywood Roosevelt Hotel, but very little that looks glamorous and appealing.

The famous Sunset Strip on Sunset Boulvard, not really within reasonable walking distance, has changed so much through the years that it is hard for today's visitors to imagine how it looked when it housed Ciro's, the Trocadero, the Mocambo, the Players, and the Cock and Bull Restaurant. You can still find the legendary Chateau Marmont Hotel, the site where Wolfgang Puck's original Spago was, and a few other places, but again, the dynamic changes that are part of Los Angeles have all taken their toll.

Gone forever is the Hollywood Canteen on Cahuenga which I frequented so much as a sailor during World War II. Also vanished is the Pike in Long Beach, another gathering spot for the U.S. Navy during the war.

Look at it this way. L.A. is big, it's vast. It changes fast. Distances are greater than they seem. City blocks seem miles long; in the San Fernando Valley, the blocks indeed stretch out endlessly like racecar lanes. For such a spread-out city, wheels are necessary. Los Angelenos seem to be born with cars in their cribs instead of bottles and pacifiers.

One needs shades, also, against the hot sun. East coast people think sunglasses are a California affectation, but they are wrong. They are a necessity.

Los Angeles is also an early-to-bed and early-to-rise town. It helps if one speaks some Spanish. Los Angelenos do stop for pedestrians and don't blow their car horns, except in dire emergencies. They are polite, patient, and helpful if you show them the same courtesy. They don't play the what-college-did-you-go-to game. They are more likely to judge you for how you present yourself to them. They love the outdoors, are adventurous, a little daring, enjoy novelty and call Iowa and Denver "back East." They refer to Los Angeles as "the Southland" and may never have been farther east than Death Valley. They usually speak well of other places like San Francisco and New York, unaware of how residents of those cities take pleasure in putting them down.

When one sails out of Los Angeles harbor into the Pacific about the last sign of civilization one sees is a long stretch in San Pedro called Ports O' Call. Sometimes when the QE2 departs, especially at night, the inhabitants of the Ports O' Call restaurant flash all the lights, turn on the loudspeaker and boom out a hearty "Bon Voyage, Queen Elizabeth" to the ship as it sails by. This gives a great lift to the passengers because this is the final touch of America they will have for a while.

On the East coast a similar event happens if you depart from Fort Lauderdale, as we did in 1994 on a long voyage to South America aboard the *Sagafjord*. An apartment house at the very end of the land has an entire floor that gets word of the departure and responds by flashing lights on and off, ringing bells, and banging pans. One knows a great send off when it happens like this.

Slow dissolve. Max Steiner music up. Fade Out into the sunset on the Pacific.

(The End, for a while)

TO SEARS IN A WHITE STRETCH LIMOUSINE

Our first stop after Los Angeles on this voyage was Honolulu on the island of Oahu in Hawaii. It was good to see the Aloha Tower at the pier looming up again, and to see the rainbow swirl of marketplace activity that surrounds it.

I always look forward to Honolulu, which I think is a very beautiful, varied, small city. I like its distinctive architecture, a kind of graceful nineteenth-century colonial style, as in the Iolani Palace, an exotic Victorian wedding cake. There are many nice parks and gardens, also, an older section, and then, heading toward impressive Diamond Head, the short (two miles) stretch of beach called Waikiki with gorgeous hotels like the pink palace, the Royal Hawaiian, and the newer Sheraton Waikiki.

The Royal Hawaiian, that *grande dame* of all Waikiki's hotels, was our choice for lunch once again. They have a large outoor cafe, partly indoors and outdoors as well, overlooking Waikiki Beach, so that one can enjoy the sun and surf-and-people watching and still remain in the shade, and the food is excellent.

After lunch, we wanted to go to Sears to buy one of those eggcrate mattresses for my wife to add to her bed in the cabin. The classily dressed doorman hailed a cab for us which turned out to be a long, white stretch limousine with a bar inside. We rode in preposterously elegant style to Sears, like the Beverly Hillbillies, made our purchase, and then took an ordinary bus back to the Aloha Tower and our ship.

On previous visits to Honolulu we had explored Pearl Harbor, seen the major sights of the city, visited some of the private homes, and done considerable walking and browsing in shops. Honolulu, of course, is the great metropolis of the island, with several universities and all the other attractions of a big city.

On the opposite side of Oahu is Waimea, a much smaller community, and near it wilder beaches such as Sunset for surfing, and more isolated resorts.

The other Hawaiian islands which we had visited previously include the big island, Hawaii, with its fantastic Volcanoes National Park, and Maui, an island mostly of expensive resorts that cater to conventions and honeymooners, but also with the charming village of La Haina (pronounced La HYNA).

We've only seen Kawai and Molokai from the ship. The islands always seem overhung with clouds and the threat of rainstorms to me. There's a feeling of the treachery of nature in the air. I never trust the weather here. I am always expecting rain and I am seldom disappointed.

Some Hawaiian memories are quasi-amusing to me now. Back in 1965, when we first visited Waikiki Beach, I remember how flattered I was when I rented a surfboard and the tanned gods in charge gave me a Big Gun, the largest one available, which I could barely manage and could not really stand up on in the water. I had to take our two daughters surfing on it with each lying flat on my back as we paddled into shore. I cut myself considerably on the sharp coral found just under the surface, a constant hazard for anybody who thinks surfing in Hawaii is a breeze.

Still, I always feel comfortable in Honolulu. It has many of the qualities I like in a city—an old quarter with a sense of tradition and a flavor of the past with interesting buildings worth preserving. It also has palm trees, long stretches of beach, boats, people doing active things like walking, swimming, boating, fishing, surfing—wholesome activity. It has a huge geographical wonder, the splendid bluff Diamond Head, marking out its landmark site on the coastline, waiting for generations of photographers to capture it in all kinds of light.

Honolulu, in addition to its nineteenth-century old world charm, also has a big city feel about it—tall buildings, smart shops, good restaurants, whizzing cars, enough to surprise and satisfy any visitor. It has a varied population, the native Polynesian islanders, for instance, always so calm and reassuring; Asians from China and Japan that give the islands greater depth in their cultural heritage, plus beachcomber refugees from the mainland in America, who are a lot more laid-back than most people, thus helping others to relax and get into a happy island mode of living.

Waikiki has two miles of beach stretching along the waterfront from Diamond Head to downtown Honolulu. There are 94 hotels, 11 of them right on the beach, making Waikiki a fairly congested area today.

On Oahu, in 1997, arriving on the QE2, I took a tour of homes set up by the Oahu Garden Club. Among the homes were Dicey Brinck's home in Mauna Willi, Sharon Fairbanks' home in Niu Valley, and Dorothy MacMillan's spectacular seaside home in Kahaluu. These beautiful homes proved how wonderfully restorative and pleasant the Hawaiian lifestyle can be. All it takes is good taste and about ten million bucks.

I thought back to our previous Hawaiian visit in 1997. We were sailing to Australia on the first leg of the QE2's world cruise. On board ship we sat at a table for six in one of the more volatile, although intriguing, social situations we have encountered.

At one end of the rectangular table sat Cicely Campkin, a charming English widow, who had recently married Dr. Victor Campkin, also a recent widower, sitting opposite her. Next to Cicely sat my wife, Rudd, and directly across from her a woman I will call Hertha, a German-born, tiny, talkative dynamo, who had escaped Hitler's holocaust, gone first to South Africa, then to New Jersey, and finally ended up in Phoenix, Arizona. I sat next to my wife in the Cicely-Rudd line and across from me was a man from New Jersey whom I'll call Cy.

Cy had been born, like his sister, with cerebral palsy, so that one had to work doubly hard to understand him sometimes because his speech had been affected. But Cy liked people and good conversation, and he was a seasoned traveler on the QE2. While Rudd, Cicely, and Victor had their own animated conversation going, Cy and I were usually locked in our dialogue with Hertha occasionally chiming in with her very definite opinions on many subjects. It turned out that Cy, for instance, was an ardent Republican. Hertha immediately attacked him on that point, for she was a confirmed Democrat. Cy also was a gambler, and nightly went into the casino on board ship as none of the rest of us ever did.

"I won $4,000 last night," Cy announced triumphantly one evening.

"How much did you spend to win that?" asked Hertha.

"About $4,500," admitted Cy.

"A-Hah! You see?" snorted Hertha.

Cy also loved his cocktails. I used to see him propped up at the bar in the Crystal Bar, chatting with the bartender.

I got to know him quite well. He told me his whole life story, but I think I was ultimately a disappointment to him because I wasn't a gambler or boozer. What I became was a referee for him and Hertha.

Incidentally, on this trip when we sailed from Los Angeles, the loudspeaker at the Port O' Call Restaurant blared out, "Ahoy, Queen Elizabeth Second, Port O' Call Restaurant wishes the captain, crew, and passengers of the Queen Elizabeth Second a safe and happy cruise around the world."

The ship responded with three loud blasts that echoed throughout the harbor. There is always an appealing mystery about such a departure into the darkness of the open channel to the Pacific Ocean, only it isn't really dark. There are myriads of lights—bell buoys blinking red and green, ships that appear like sudden diamond points of light, odd licking voices of waves washing against the side of the ship or airplanes taking off and cutting through the night sky like giant moths, headed out to make circular turns over the sea.

The first port we arrived at on that voyage was Ensenada in Baja California, another Mexican town like Tijuana, with colorful, active, ticky-tacky shops, except that this one was a port town. And, typically, passengers were confronted by the usual mothers with their children thrust out in front of them begging for money. However, that was 1997. The last time I was in Mexico, this unfortunate practice seemed to have disappeared.

In Ensenada there is a park there near the harbor with outsize sculptures of three men, one of whom is Benito Juarez. I remembered that Paul Muni and Bette Davis had appeared in the Warner Brothers movie about the great Mexican peasant leader's life back in 1939.

After Ensenada, we had four days at sea. We did not see a single ship in the Pacific enroute to Hilo. The Pacific is a beautiful dark lapis lazuli blue and quite placid, but the QE2 cuts through it at around 25 knots average, so the swells are quite apparent.

For the arrival at Hilo, lights appeared like a thin, diamond bracelet in the night straight ahead. A few planes took off from the airport. Then we landed, went through a breakwater with tug boats pushing us, to dock at the pier.

I took the Volcanoes National Park Tour. The guide was "Cousin Thomas" who told us about his six children, sang songs incessantly, repeated bad jokes, and made a shameless play for our sympathy and gratuities, very annoying to many.

I found Volcanoes National Park, an extra-ordinary and very accessible place. We made a circular tour around the Kilauea caldera, stopping first on Crater Rim Drive to see hundreds of steam vents blowing up through the ground. When you put your hand into the steam near the ground, you can feel how extremely hot they are.

The landscape there looks like that of a blighted land—low, scalded vegetation, but with sudden, unexpected rain showers. This is the wet side of Hawaii. Kona is on the dry side on the opposite shore of Hawaii.

Looking around, Cousin Thomas explained that astronauts are brought to Volcanoes National Park for part of their training because the terrain resembles that of the moon.

Next we walked to the Kilauea overlook, where we got a panoramic view of the crater. Kilauea is 4,000 feet above sea level. Shifting fog and clouds change the view almost every second. We were lucky to have gotten so clear a view.

Also there is the Jagger Museum with displays and information on volcanoes. One of the guides explained that there are three basic types of volcanoes: The caldera type is like a cherry pie, he said, when the top crust bubbles and boils and finally blows, splattering bits everywhere.

Then we went around the Southwest Rift to the Halema' uma 'u crater overlook where we gazed down into the face of the small crater. Flowers had been placed there by natives, who also built little cairns of rocks as part of their worship to the goddess Pele.

As we headed toward the Thurston Lava Tube, the landscape changed again. First it appeared like a sheet of over-baked brownies in the oven—brown, grey, and broken crusts. We also saw huge fissures in the earth caused by the frequent earthquakes that precede eruption. This is also the reason houses in the area have corrugated iron roofs—because they shift easily, and thus safely, when an earthquake starts.

The driver of our bus had us close our eyes as we approached Pu' u Pua'i and then open them to find ourselves in a vast rain forest, looking more like something out of Africa or Brazil. Enormous philodendron vines, jungle growth, huge fern fronds, etc., very beautiful, tangled, mysterious, faintly sinister.

Then we disappeared into a lava flow tube, totally dark, underground, with dripping water from the ceiling and little pools of water underfoot that you had to ford. Lava flows through these tunnels into the sea whenever an eruption occurs, which, we hoped, would not be while we were exploring the tube.

Back in town again, we stopped first at Hilo Hatties, a clothing store in a shopping center with Sears, Woolworths, Liberty House, and, coming soon, a Wal Mart.

Later, with Rudd, who had taken a different tour, I went into old town Hilo which looked like a run-down, once pretty, port town. Many shops were empty. A bus driver explained to us that at a certain age these buildings will be restored by federal funds and that some buildings were just reaching that age then, but, he admitted, the shopping center typically had taken away a lot of business.

Once there had been sugar plantations on Hawaii, but now only one was left, soon to go. The new cash crop is macademia nuts. The big rival for macademia nuts is South Africa. Hawaii has a fairly large unemployment rate.

The big resort area at Kona is another economic hope for this largest of the Hawaiian islands.

Cousin Thomas made sure we understood that he was a full-blooded Hawaiian, only 8,000 of them left now, a small percentage of the total population.

On the next day of the 1997 cruise, I signed up for a Circle Tour of Oahu with a guide named Ed:

We toured the city of Honolulu first, which has three distinct sections—the Old City, largely Chinatown, from the 1870s, because the bubonic plague devastated the population before that date; then the business district; and finally, the government area. Ed discussed Hawaiian history and rulers—Queen Liliuokalani; Queen Emma, King Kamehameha. Honolulu appeared very beautiful to me—green parks, tidy streets, attractive plantation-like buildings. Nice landscaping.

We crossed to the other side of the island, northeast, to the town of Kanohe in a rather beautiful setting on a bay. Then to Waihane, where a large rock in the water is called Chinaman's Hat. Then to the Polynesian Cultural Center, run by Mormons, and the Mormon Temple itself in a gleaming all-white Shangri-La style architecture.

We lunched that day at the Turtle Bay Hilton in a dramatic location on Kahuku Point. Ocean crashing on rocks. Nice sandy beach, A wild, spectacular resort.

Then we drove to the famous North shore surfing beachs—Sunset Beach and Waimea Bay. Ed knew all the important breaks—the Pipeline, Marijuana Beach—a vicarious day in the surf and we didn't even have to get wet. Way to go, dude!

Our bus then crossed through the middle of the island on a plateau set among the mountains. We saw the legendary pineapple plantations of Dole and Del Monte, but learned that nothing is canned in Hawaii anymore. Labor is too expensive. The pineapple is now sent to Indonesia or Thailand instead.

We traveled along the road between the two mountain ranges of Waianae and Koolau, the path through which Japanese bombers flew to take out the airfields and Pearl Harbor in 1941's surprise attack. We passed the infamous Schofield Barracks which I knew from James Jones' brilliant novel *From Here to Eternity*.

Then we went to the moving spectre of Pearl Harbor itself. We saw the fleet in mothballs and the *Arizona* memorial. I was astonished at the great number of Japanese tourists who were also there.

Ed spoke movingly about the battleship *Utah* which he said was never raised. It was very difficult coming face to face with this reminder of how war slams into one's life and of the treachery of nations.

Back in Honolulu again, I asked Ed if he had favored statehood for Hawaii. He said only 51% of the Hawaiians voted for it. Ed voted against it. I wondered about this because much of what I admired in Hawaii were the aspects that differed from those on the mainland.

Rudd and I also visited Hawaii in March and April of 1998. Hawaii was on the itinerary of the *Vistafjord's* voyage to the South Pacific.

On this trip we stopped first at La Haina in Maui. A charming village, what one expects a Hawaiian town should look like (if one believes all those glamorous Paramount movies of one's youth), La Haina was once a sailors' port where the ladies were as shady as the palm trees are today. We took a tour that went from La Haina with its dry mesquite brush up to a more mountainous area where rain falls more regularly. Maui was in a serious drought condition down below, we found out.

Our first stop was a sugar plantation, after which we went to a very sharp mountain called the Needle. This was at a park where several rivers meet. We had a steep climb up to the lookout station, which was not too impressive, possibly because of the severe drought.

We stopped next at a tropical plantation with picturesque windmills and interesting foliage and also had shopping time at Whalers' Village in a big hotel resort area. This featured incongruous shops like

Ferragamo, Gucci—upscale, trendy. Why would you want to bring a big city lifestyle to an island like this? If one looked beyond all this glitter and largesse, one could see the coastline offering simpler pleasures. Some people even spotted whales breeching in the ocean.

We went next to Kona on the big island of Hawaii. The town again is attractive, well maintained, and is attempting to preserve its heritage. There is a big Congregational church in town, studded with lava rock, another reminder of the strong influence of Christian missionaries in these islands.

We went part of the way up on famous Mauna Loa (which is 13,677 feet high) to a higher location with better vegetation. This is the dry side of Hawaii. Hilo, on the opposite shore where we had been before, is the wet side.

We visited a fragrant coffee plantation first, and next went to a sacred place of refuge, called Pu'uhona o Honaunau, now a national historical park with interesting native Hawaiian huts, ruins of temples, a great wall, stone relics, and 180 acres of what remains of the palace grounds, beautifully situated by the sea. This became a national historic park in 1961 and the idea was to restore it to its appearance as it was in the late 1700s.

After that we went to St. Benedict's Painted Church, hand-painted by a priest-friend of Father Damien (of Molokai and the lepers' colony fame), Father Velgeie from Belgium.

Later, Rudd and I walked leisurely through the shopping part of town and the port area before returning to the ship. We were moored near the *Independence*, remembered by us from our New York days, but a ship which now travels among the Hawaiian islands.

On this big island also is the Volcanoes National Park which I visited for the second time, but this time with Rudd. It was especially nice that I had been there before and could point out to her some of the sights I thought were distinctive.

Volcanoes is very large and impressive, more interesting to me than Yosemite or Yellowstone and on a par with the Grand Canyon. We walked around the Kilauea Caldera and down among the Thurston lava tube to the black sand beach. Some people still leave offerings of flowers and fruits on the caldera's rim to appease the goddess Pele, and at times steam rises from vents in the ground, which could burn one seriously should one reach one's hands in. Deep in the caldera one can see the bright red and yellow of flames.

Volcanoes is unique. Neither Etna nor Vesuvius offers such a strange moonscape that one can walk around in and see the tremendous power Nature has to change the face of things.

I think this great national park is Hawaii's rarest treasure and a traveler's happiest find in these islands.

ON SHIPBOARD

"There is nothing—absolutely nothing—half so much worth doing as simply messing about in boats, . . . or with boats . . . . In or out of 'em, it doesn't matter."

Kenneth Grahame

The *Queen Elizabeth 2* was built in the John Brown Shipyard on the banks of the Clyde River in Scotland in the 1960s and officially launched September 20, 1967 by Queen Elizabeth II who said "I name this ship *Queen Elizabeth the Second*," meaning that it was not named after Her Majesty but was the second ship to bear that name. The first ship, however, *was* named after her mother who was then Queen Elizabeth.

The QE2, as it is called, was specially designed to pass through the Panama Canal which was 110 feet wide. The QE2 is 105 feet and 2.5 inches wide, so it just scrapes through. The QE2 is 963 feet long. The ship was designed by James Gardner, CBE, and Dennis Lennon in cooperation with Cunard's Chief Naval Architect, Dan Wallace.

The Cunard Line, which built the QE2, was responsible for over 150 ships from 1840 to 1930. In 1936 Cunard White Star built the *Queen Mary*, now in Long Beach, California, and in 1938 the first *Queen Elizabeth*.

The very first passenger on the QE2 was Prince Charles, son of the Queen and Prince Philip. Other distinguished persons who have sailed on the ship include the Queen and Prince Philip, Princess Diana, Nelson Mandela, Julie Andrews, Richard Burton,

Elizabeth Taylor, Bill Cosby, Bob Hope, Mick Jagger, Elton John, Paul Newman, Meryl Streep, John Travolta, The Sultan of Brunei, and President George W. Bush.

Other interesting information: The crew numbers 921. The number of passengers varies from 1200 to 1700. 80 private cars can be transported on the ship. There are 6 restaurants. The kitchens are set up to feed over 3,000 people in 2 1/2 hours if necessary. There is the largest hospital afloat with 2 doctors and 6 nurses in attendance. There are kennels for animals, swimming pools, shops, launderettes, and air-conditioning throughout. There are also 22 elevators to transport people up and down 13 decks. The ship is equipped with stabilizers for rough weather and has achieved a speed of 33.11 knots, but usually cruises at between 20-28 knots.

The QE2 has had 19 Masters since its launching. The Master on our world cruise was Captain R. W. Warwick, son of the very first Master, Commodore W. E. Warwick. At Southampton, Captain Paul Wright took over for the Atlantic crossing to New York. Both men were also very visible on the ship and entertained frequently at social functions. Warwick is shy and reserved, very gentlemanly. Wright, more outgoing perhaps, throws great, convivial parties.

Other officers on board include the Staff Captain, the Chief Officer, the Security Officer, the Chief Engineer, the Hotel Manager, the Cruise Director, the Principal Medical Officer, and all their support staffs.

The QE2, like all ocean liners, is in reality a large floating village. One recalls the comment actress Beatrice Lillie is reported to have made on the *Queen Mary* in the 1930s. She asked the Captain, "Pardon me, but what time does this place get to New York?"

E-Mail from Verna Rudd Kenvin, Cabin no. 4127
To: Brooke, Heather
Date: Thursday, January 25

Our stay in Honolulu ended with a lovely departure, complete with dancers, music, singers, and ginger blossoms thrown onto the ship from a circling helicopter. There was also a large, gorgeous rainbow over the mountains as we sailed out of the harbor.

It just started to rain as we arrived back at the ship from our lunch at the Royal Hawaiian Hotel and our shopping at Sears, where we bought a foam bed pad for me. The latter gave us some laughs because the taxi which took us from the hotel to Sears in the HUGE shopping center was a white stretch limousine. (I did not want to overdo the walking and Papa was feeling a bit tired.)

The luncheon was very nice, not too expensive, and we were at a table overlooking the lovely beach and the beautifully colored ocean. This area at Waikiki is so built up from the time in 1965 when we all were there and Papa tried to surf, but the landscaping around the hotel is cleverly planted so that it blocks out most of the tall buildings. You just see one high-rise hotel in front of the famous mountain, Diamond Head.

After I bought my foam mattress (which helped last night) we went down to the street and got a bus back to the ship for a dollar each, a better bargain.

We were fortunate in having good weather in Hawaii. It was hot, but not too much so. Today, we are at sea with rather a lot of motion. The captain just finished saying it will be like that all day. It makes it hard to get a good night's rest, really, but one can always nap. That's what's so good about ships. . . .

Lots of love from both of us.

Mom

STARKIST AND SADIE

"Pago-Pago is about the rainiest place in the Pacific. You see, those hills and that bay, they attract the water. One expects rain at this time of the year anyway."

W. Somerset Maugham

It is pronounced "Pango Pango," but that doesn't bother the British, including the captain of the QE2, who authoritatively pronounces it "Paygo Paygo," thus thoroughly confusing those who think the British way is necessarily the correct way.

Pago Pago has an attractive harbor, with the exotic-looking Rainmaker Hotel well-situated on a point of land visible to passengers as the ship enters.

Pago Pago is the setting of W. Somerset Maugham's famous short story "Rain," which has the Reverend Davidson, against his will, involved in a steamy affair with Miss Sadie Thompson. It was made into a successful stage play starring the actress Jeanne Eagels and has at least twice been made into motion pictures with first, Joan Crawford playing Sadie, and later, Ava Gardner. The Rainmaker Hotel has a Sadie Thompson bar and the town itself has a claustrophobic feel about it, fostering a strong sense that in the monsoon season, another recreation of the Reverend Davidson-Sadie story could again take place.

Since it was hot and humid there, Rudd and I headed first for the hotel where we polished off a couple of coca colas instead of whiskey and hoped to watch the Baltimore Ravens and New York Giants in the football Superbowl on a big screen.

The big plant in town is the Starkist Tuna Canning plant. Near it a new breakwater is being built.

The town seems very rundown to me, reminding me of St. Croix in the U.S. Virgin Islands. Most of the buildings have flat roofs and do not look very substantial.

The Rainmaker Hotel at one end, for instance, seems faded and not formerly elegant. It has a huge chandelier made of shells in the lobby, the damp, musty Sadie Thompson bar, a crescent-shaped beach, individual bungalows with modern thatched roofs, and also a motel with beach-facing rooms boasting outside glass walls. The beach looks inviting and pleasant and guests were happily swimming.

Obviously, the economy is not very prosperous, but the Samoan people themselves impressed me as being friendly, good-natured, guileless, and trustworthy. Often, they are fairly large people with cheerful, open faces. Ethnically, most are of Polynesian ancestry, and some perhaps are a little envious of the huge success of their neighbors to the north in the Hawaiian islands.

The harbor at Pago Pago is a good one. Quite a few boats there. The climate is perpetually hot and humid in this location just south of the Equator, and probably this difficult climate makes it less attractive to visitors than Hawaii.

Pago Pago is located on an island called Tutuila, about seventeen miles long and four miles wide. It is the largest of the seven islands that comprise American Samoa, all of them smaller, so one can understand why I call it slightly claustrophobic.

There is another Samoa which is a separate, independent nation. I have heard it referred to as "Western Samoa" or "German Samoa." In American

Samoa, there are about 60,000 inhabitants and the Samoans do have a representative in the U.S. Congress.

Somerset Maugham visited Pago Pago in 1916 and wrote his famous short story after that visit. Many of the houses still have thatched roofs, easily replaceable in case of damage. Christian churches are also very much a staple of town life here, as they are in Hawaii. The first missionary was an Englishman, Reverend John Williams, who arrived in Tutuila in 1832.

In 1997, on the QE2 again, Rudd and I visited American Samoa and traveled out into the small villages in the countryside. For a population of about 60,000, there are an inordinate number of churches—Latter Day Saints, Catholic, Pentacostal. Families are important in community life, which is is strongly patriarchal. The village elders meet in thatched fales propped up by poles, and, in these large huts, they hash out village problems.

Throughout the island, people live in typical Polynesian homes with corrugated iron roofs that shift easily during strong windstorms. We went to a kava ceremony in a village fale where we participated in their singing, dancing, and ceremonial customs.

If Pago-Pago appears a bit worn, so do the island roads. It is nowhere a prosperous-looking place, but the climate and meteorology clearly determine the slower, more laid-back pace of life on the islands.

In handicrafts, Samoans weave mats, print large patterns on cloth, and make things from wood. In business, in addition to tuna canning, there is a copra industry, and a large U.S. military contingent.

I liked Samoa mostly because of its pleasant people, who are not too Americanized, but natural and relaxed, so that one enjoys their company.

A small drama took place as the QE2 maneuvered its way out of the harbor. A little boy, perhaps six years old, standing on the wharf, kept waving incessantly to the ship and hopping up and down in his own enthusiastic choreography. He followed the ship to the farthest point, still jumping and waving. A woman on the ship impulsively tossed him a yellow floral lei which he gathered up hungrily and hung around his neck. He waved exuberantly his thanks to her. It seemed as though this departure must have mattered greatly to him. I wondered how many ships' sailings he had attended and how long he would have to wait before he could put out to sea himself.

ON SHIPBOARD

Tourists are people who sign up for quick looks, grab a few souvenirs, take a few photographs to prove they've been there, and head home fast before their neighbors can get to where they've already been.

Travelers, on the other hand, set out in search of something—new people, new lands, new cultures, and understand that they may never reach home again.

METHODISTS IN ORCHIDS

Fiji is a republic and part of the British Commonwealth. It is made up of over 320 islands, only about 100 of which are inhabited. The total population is about 750,000 and the majority of Fijians live on the largest island, Viti Levu.

The Fijian natives are a tall, strong, handsome people with dark skins like burnished ebony. They closely resemble Africans in their muscular physiques, but most anthropologists believe the original Fijians migrated to these South Pacific islands from Southeast Asia by way of Indonesia.

At any rate, they are an impressive-looking people. The Fijians themselves love to remind visitors humorously that they were cannibals well into the nineteenth century. A famous Fijian story tells of the notorious British captain, William Bligh, and how, after the mutiny took place on his ship *The Bounty*, he and some of the survivors of the mutiny tried to land in Fiji in 1789 and were chased away by Fijians rowing after them in a fleet of canoes.

Fijian canoes themselves are one of the wonders of Fijian industry. They produced double-hulled outrigger canoes that were well over 100 feet long and could carry as many as 200 sailors at a clip. One can picture Captain Bligh's enormous surprise at encountering such a formidable armada in the middle of the South Pacific.

In addition to the native Fijians, more recent immigrants have included groups from India and China.

The protection from Great Britain came in the nineteenth-century when a Fijian chief, Thakombau, had trouble maintaining order and asked that Fiji be taken over by the United States, Great Britain, or Germany. Great Britain won out, and today, in Suva, the capital city, the usual British trademarks are found— Victoria Parade is the main street; Albert Park is the leading park, complete with bowling greens; Queen's Road, Queen Elizabeth Drive, and Prince's Landing are other leading place names in town.

In 1997 on the QE2 we sailed into Suva's harbor and began our tour at Prince's Landing. Here is what I wrote in my journal:

It rained almost constantly during our entire visit.

Suva and surroundings are not very impressive. The city, with its population of about 120,000, resembles a run-down Caribbean town. The landscape is not nearly so interesting as that of Samoa, nor so well tended. The unpleasant image of the trashbin of the Pacific occurred to me, for that is what much of it looked like. I saw no beautiful beaches, blue water, nor pleasant prospects. Perhaps these are found in a few resorts catering to those with plenty of money.

A tacky police band played for us on arrival and departure—well-meaning, perhaps, and cordial, but not much together.

We went on tour to Orchid Island which is a Fijian cultural center, including houses, temples, flora and fauna of the island. I learned that the Fijians were cannibals for a long time. They used to fatten up men and boys only and then imprison them alive in building timbers. "But," the chief of the village reassured us, "Not anymore. Today we are all Methodists. We believe in one man, one wife, one god."

On Orchid Island, we were able to watch various demonstrations—how to catch a land crab or land lobster, for instance, and how to trap a mongoose or gecko. We saw a boa constrictor, an iguana, a weaving demonstration, and sampled local food.

We also saw the traditional kava ceremony performed in one of their thatched halls with pandanus leaves on the roof. One of the passengers from the ship was selected as the honored guest and had to be the first to drink from the bowl. Then the people performed songs and dances very handsomely. The people were friendly and gracious. The visit to Orchid Island was illuminating.

An interesting, perhaps ironic sidelight: In the harbor the QE2 was docked next to a United States' destroyer.

On our current voyage in 2001, we could not go into Suva because of some political turbulence taking place there, so the QE2 headed for the other side of Viti Levu and the port of Lautoka.

The television actor, Raymond Burr, known for his *Perry Mason* and *Ironside* shows, had at one time owned a large compound near Lautoka, where he raised orchids and anthuriums. His former home, now owned by Don and Aileen Burness, was the setting for our visit, complete with tea and a talk by Aileen Burness. We sat in the spacious living room of a large wooden plantation house, while Mrs. Burness discussed various articles of furniture, antiques, and decorations and Raymond Burr's sojourns there. It seemed a pleasant, relaxed way of life, and we enjoyed the spectacular gardens and the leafy environment.

After that, we visited another Fijian village, and, on this visit, I walked around independently, stopping to photograph and chat with women, families, anybody who ventured out to talk to me. Once again, I was impressed with the friendliness and intelligence of the inhabitants. Four women sitting on the ground under a tree pulled me down to join them for a few moments while they laughingly told me their names and asked where I was from and what was it like sailing on the QE2.

As for the city of Lautoka itself, it has a large Indian population, originally brought to Fiji as indentured servants. This gives Lautoka a different flavor from that of Suva. There is a large Hindu temple in town, for instance, and the two big manufacturing plants are a large sugar refinery and a distillery. The city has tall, jagged mountains around it, giving it a distinctive appearance.

Also on Viti Levu is another city, Nadi, (pronounced Nandi), near which the international airport is located. Travelers to and from the United States and/or New Zealand or Australia often stop for refueling at this airport.

Fijians, in contrast to the Polynesians, seem more energetic to me. Or maybe their faster pace just runs closer to my own.

ON SHIPBOARD

"We joined the navy to see the world,
And what did we see—we saw the sea."

Irving Berlin

On the Pacific Ocean, you can sit for days on the deck, looking at the sapphire blue sea, without seeing land, fish, birds, or another ship for what seems an eternity. It set me thinking about a sailor's life and the proverbial seven seas. I realized that, after this trip, Rudd and I will have sailed far more than just seven. Here they are, as dramatic and funny in their way as Danny Kaye's song "Tchaikowsky" was with its litany of Russian composers:

Pacific Ocean, Tasman Sea, Southern Ocean, Indian Ocean, Sulu Sea, South China Sea, East China Sea, Japan Inland Sea, Andaman Sea, Arabian Sea, Red Sea, Mediterranean Sea, Atlantic Ocean, North Sea, Irish Sea, Adriatic Sea, Aegean Sea, Sea of Marmara, Black Sea, Caribbean Sea, Celebes Sea, Laccadive Sea, Ionian Sea, Tyrrhenian Sea, Balearic Sea, Ligurian Sea, Albaran Sea, and the Sea of Cortez.

That makes 28 seas for us, and does not include all the gulfs, lakes, bays, inlets, sounds, and rivers.

E-Mail from Verna Rudd Kenvin, Cabin no. 4127
To: Heather, Brooke
Date: Thursday, February 1

. . .   Papa has had a bad cold since we left Hawaii. He stayed in the room and had room service, but he was able to go ashore at Pago Pago. We did not have a tour, so we just took a brief taxi ride around town and went to the Rainmaker Hotel for a coke and to investigate the so-called "large television screen" for the Superbowl game. It turned out to be only the size of a normal tv. We didn't return for the game. It was just as well.

P also had to miss the captain's dinner for passengers on the whole world cruise—425 in all, but parties for about 25 each time. I went and it was a lot of fun. Excellent food and some delightful people.

At Fiji, P was well enough to go on the tour to Raymond Burr's former home. This was an interesting trip with an excellent Fijian guide. The Fijians are such friendly people. . . .

We have had the opportunity to see some good movies on our room tv, and we have attended more good concerts in the theatre. Otherwise, the entertainment aboard is a bit weak.

We have had good weather all along, except for a few rough times. Often VERY HOT and VERY HUMID. No problems though. . . .

We are looking forward to talking with you on your Saturday. Lots of love, and hugs and kisses.

Mom

E-Mail from Verna Rudd Kenvin, Cabin no. 4127
To: Rob, Brooke, Heather
Date: February 1

. . . We are enjoying the trip very much despite Roger's cold, which is almost finished, and my knee problem, better on some days, but not on others. The roll of the ship does not help. Still, it is a wonderful ship and a great place to take it easy. Since we have been on it many times before, we do not feel we need to go to every lecture. Besides, most of them are televised to the cabin all day long, so you can catch bits and pieces and still get things done in your cabin, such as signing one's travelers' checks, which I discovered I had not done. . . .

Tomorrow night, our February 3rd, we are going to a very posh dinner in Auckland for all World Cruise Club members. Of course, formal dress. . . .

Rudd

AUNT AGNES, MAORI TONGUES, AND THE KIEHL OF MANY COLORS

"I want, by understanding myself, to understand others.
I want to be all that I am capable of becoming."

Katherine Mansfield

Almost every nation one stops at in the Pacific seems to be composed of many islands; only the map fuses them into one place.

New Zealand is no exception. Like Hawaii, it is actually a collection of islands, although the two biggest ones, called North Island and South Island dominate. The total population is about 3.6 million, of which 75% live on North Island, predominantly in the two cities of Auckland and Wellington, the capital. This is a warm island with a subtropical climate.

South Island, on the other hand, has the spectacular Southern Alps, giving it a Swiss-Norwegian aspect. It contains charming cities like Christchurch and Dunedin, and the beautiful Milford Sound. It is more rural, typifying the predominance of sheep-raising, which in New Zealand means that sheep outnumber human beings.

On our first visit there in 1997, we docked first at Auckland, located on an isthmus above the center of North Island. Auckland is called "The City of Sails" and it was easy to see why. Auckland's extensive harbor has the Pacific Ocean on one side and the Waitemata Harbor on the other, which gives out into the Tasman Sea. Auckland is rightly a sailor's paradise. The Westhaven Boat Harbor is perhaps the largest yacht basin in the world. Aucklanders enjoy their sails.

Other odd facts about Auckland: The city is built on the remains of about sixty volcanoes, making its geography of hills and water extremely dramatic and appealing. It is also an extensive city, both physically, and in population, numbering over one million inhabitants. About 17% of these are Polynesians, the greatest concentration of them anywhere in the world.

For me, personally, Auckland was where my Aunt Agnes, whom I never met, lived after she emigrated there from Ireland early in the twentieth century. Agnes Flood was the sister of my grandmother, Mary Flood Macdonald, and they parted company when Agnes went to live in New Zealand and Mary in the United States.

When I was a little boy of five or six, Agnes would write my mother a long letter every Christmas detailing her life in New Zealand which my mother would read to her children eager to hear all her news, and then at New Year's we would listen on the radio to the scratchy, distant sound of Big Ben in London tolling in the new year. That was our set holiday ritual up to World War II. Agnes had married and become Mrs. John Bright and had a family. That I knew.

When I finally arrived in Auckland in 1997, both my grandmother and mother had died, and I assumed Agnes probably had, too. But I thought perhaps her children might still be there. To my surprise, when I checked the name "Bright" in the Auckland telephone directory, I found hundreds of them. Apparently, the name is as common as "Johnson" in the United States. At any rate, I had Aunt Agnes in mind all the time I spent in Auckland and decided that she had made a very wise choice.

In 1997, when we arrived in Auckland, it was raining. This in an outdoorsy city where one out of six persons owns a boat—the City of Sails. We spent the day riding on a bus into the beautiful New Zealand countryside, taking in the long, blue mountain ranges, rolling green farms, many with windbreaks or hedgerows of one sort or another. Naturally, we saw lots of sheep, although New Zealand is trying to switch over to cattle since sheep raising for wool or meat is now not too profitable.

We went over the Bombay Hills into the Waikato River Valley where we stopped at Huntly for a morning break. A large electric plant, looking slightly anachronistic, loomed up nearby.

Then we climbed into the Makamu Mountain range through forests fairly tropical-looking, somewhat reminiscent of those in Samoa. We finally reached Rotorua after going through a strange landscape of calderas with little bumpy volcano tops. Lots of steam was escaping and there was the strong, pungent smell of sulphur in the air. Rotorua sits on the edge of a lake. The place is both a celebrated spa, with the usual hotels and resorts, and it also is a major center of Maori culture.

We had lunch at a large hotel where a Maori troupe performed songs and dances for us, including the Maoris' war chant where men jump out, stick out their tongues, and bulge out their eyes at their opponents. It is supposed to be frightening, but I found it funny.

Next, we went through the Whakarewarewa Thermal Reserve, stopping first at the Maori Arts and Crafts Institute where we saw wood-carving, weaving, and other demonstrations and were talked to by a young Maori man with attitude who loudly referred to us as "QE2 people" in a snide manner, ignoring the fact that some passengers had come great distances because they were genuinely interested in learning about Maori life and culture and did not regard themselves or their own cultures as superior to it. Youth has its own arrogance and stereotypes, I guess.

After this, we walked through the preserve itself with its sulphurous steam geysers, bubbling pools, and unusual moon-like landscape. We found ourselves in a living Maori Village. The children dived for coins and dollar bills into the healing waters which were like a swimming hole to them. Tom Sawyer and Huckleberry Finn redivivus!

Then we were driven to Rainbow Springs, an organized preserve, with rainbow trout, emus, kiwi birds, all prettily arranged. For the kiwis, one has to go into a dark cave to see them.

From there we went to something called an agrodome on a farm where we saw an excellent demonstration of varieties of sheep, sheep shearing, sheep herding. The agrodome itself was a huge barn building with a horseshoe-like stage arranged in tiers with railings. The superb guide told us about different kinds of sheep with names like Suffolk, Dorset, etc. and his point was that sheep actually are smart and can learn; they are not dumb animals, as many people think. He easily proved his point in his demonstration, bringing on sheep that literally performed and seemed to think. It was one of the most fascinating animal demonstrations I have ever seen.

On the way back, we stopped at another farm for dinner, this spread being about 184 acres with 250 head of cattle. The name was "Longlands Farm," run by Kenny Simpson and his wife. This was a charming, comfortable place. We dined with our tablemates from the QE2, Dr. and Mrs. Victor Campkin and really appreciated the good food and splendid hospitality of the Simpsons.

In 2001, we had two days in Auckland. On the first day we first went up the Sky Tower, which is similar to the Space Needle in Seattle, a tall tower that affords excellent views of the vast Auckland landscape. Then we went to Albert Park and the Auckland Domain with its imposing marble War Memorial Museum housing Maori artifacts, including their large canoes (one was 82 feet long), masks, and artwork. I walked outside and looked around, watched a cricket match on a cricket pitch for a while, and looked at Auckland University, which is near Albert Park. There are 28,000 students there of whom 6000 are international.

Auckland, like all New Zealand, is remarkably clean and attractive. The country looks prosperous, and, indeed, I was told the unemployment rate is 8%.

On the second day, Saturday, February 3, 2001, we were invited by Cunard to attend the annual formal dinner of the Cunard World Cruise Club which was to be held at the Ti Papa Equestrian Center twenty miles away in South Auckland. People flew in from all parts of the world for this event.

We were bussed out there in our evening finery and found ourselves in this immaculate equestrian center with the cleanest stables I have ever seen. While drinking champagne before dinner, we watched an outdoor dressage and jumping demonstration by a magnificent bay horse named Curious George and his lady rider.

Then, when it was time for dinner, a red-coated trumpeter tooted out a rousing call to chow and Curious George and the lady led us into a huge chamber set with a stage and many round tables, all with place cards, where the actual dinner was held.

The entertainment was Maoris performing their vivid songs and dances, and the food and drink were so superb and plentiful that there were reports of some drunken disasters on the part of a few passengers on the way back to the ship.

Our table, No. 17, had a typical mix of people—my wife and me from California, a loquacious but cordial Dutch bachelor, 68 years old, Jacobus de Rover from the Hague, Netherlands. A quiet couple from Michigan, both wearing sunglasses. A blonde Englishwoman, part of the ship's staff, and the real stand-out, Arno-Walter Kiehl, a German now living in Pulau Pinang, Malaysia.

Kiehl was a big man, reminiscent of the Washington Redskins football player Sonny Jurgensen. He had a great shock of bright red hair and wore a boldly blue, raw silk tunic suit with a fuschia handkerchief. He told us he always bought raw silk in Thailand and had it made up into these striking tunic suits in different colors. He also explained the absence of his wife, who was thirty-eight years younger than he was. She had left him, he said, and taken their son, now ten years old, back to Germany because she could not stand the Muslim life in Pulau Pinang. Kiehl said, "The bitch hasn't let me see my son for six years."

From that night on, I noticed Kiehl whenever I saw him on the ship. In the dining room, I looked around from Rudd's and my table for two and saw Kiehl, always sitting totally alone at a table set for six. But Kiehl was always the sole occupant. This seemed odd since the ship was often full to capacity.

On successive nights I would see Kiehl first in canary yellow, then in hot pink, Kelly green, chalk white, everything but a proper black tuxedo, same seat, same table, with two or three waiters dancing attendance upon him.

During the daytime, I would see Kiehl in the Golden Lion Pub on the Main deck, nursing a large schooner of beer and usually seated opposite another man also with a beer. Both seemed engrossed in their conversation and drinks.

Only in the last week of the voyage, between Marseille and Southampton, where Kiehl got off, did his dining room table situation change. Now his beer-drinking crony joined him for dinner at his table.

Kiehl was one of those walking dramas one sometimes runs into among passengers on a cruise. He was not in any way effeminate, but taciturn and solid, a bull of a man, quite secure in himself and in his colorful, if very unusual wardrobe. He never said so, but I surmised that he was heading for Germany to try to see his son. I am sure he succeeded.

———————

On the 1997 trip, we also visited Wellington, which is the capital of New Zealand. Much smaller than Auckland, the population is about 350,000 people, Wellington is quieter and more manageable, reminding many of San Francisco because it is steeply hilly around the harbor and many Wellingtonians prize a home with a view. Wellington, like San Francisco, is quite windy, but I was told the winds can sometimes be extreme here.

I particularly enjoyed the individualistic, colorfully-painted houses rising up in the hills from the harbor. On one of these streets, the great short story writer, Katherine Mansfield was born. She lived on Tinakori Road. Sean, our guide, pointed out her former home to me.

We also saw Old St. Paul's Church on Mulgrave Street, built in 1864, by a vicar who was also an architect, Frederick Thatcher.

New Zealand's Parliament on Molesworth Street, with its three different buildings was an architectural curiosity—the main building, which is the Legislature, dating from 1922, the Gothic General Assembly Library (1897), and the Executive Wing, called "the Beehive." These three contiguous buildings constitute almost a history of architecture in the city.

Other city attractions I noted were the grand brick railway station, the Park Royal Hotel, and Lambton Quay, the main commercial street running along the waterfront, now with added reclaimed land added to it. It looked smart, bustling, an exciting shopping street, with many flowers planted along it. Wellington streets appeared very neat and clean, the people friendly.

Up above Lambton Quay we went up Kelburn Hill to the Botanic Gardens and the extensive Lady Norwood Rose Garden and Begonia House. Again, the views from up there are superb.

Finally, we went up Mount Victoria, surely the *pièce de resistance* of views in Wellington. One can see, for miles around, a vivid panorama of an ideal environment for any human being.

What interested me especially on top of Mount Victoria was a large stone memorial to an American, Admiral Richard Byrd. The reason for it is that he made New Zealand his main base for his Antarctica and South Pole explorations and the New Zealanders never forgot him.

Nor would I ever forget this green and pleasant land, partly mine now too through the spirit of Aunt Agnes and my having touched down at last in the land she chose.

ON SHIPBOARD

"Where there is music there can be no evil."

Miguel Cervantes

Monday, February 5, 2001, we attended a classical music concert in the theatre. Three young musicians performed. This was one of six concerts they would give, all of which we attended after we heard them the first time. We got to know them a bit personally, also, as one does aboard ship, and two of them were having an interesting story unfold in their private lives.

Daniel Vaiman, the talented pianist, had been born in Latvia in 1978, but since 1989 he and his family had lived in Israel. His original teacher was his mother, Dina Joffee, but in 1994 he studied at the Purcell School of Music in London and then at the Royal Academy of Music from which he graduated in 2000. He is both an exceptionally gifted solo performer and an unusually sensitive accompanist.

In this concert, he played Franz Liszt's "La Campanella" superbly, and in other programs he played Scherzos, Nocturnes, and Etudes by Chopin with equal brilliance. It is rare that one so young should be this versatile and accomplished.

He has given concerts in the United States, Israel, the Far East, and South America. He currently is living in Germany.

At the piano, Danny, a stocky young man, usually wearing basic black, had a face like a fun-loving gnome, suppressing mirth. He told me he had trouble remembering opuses when I asked him about one of the Chopin compositions he played.

Katy MacKintosh, on the other hand, is a Glaswegian from Scotland. She learned to play the piano at two and the oboe at fourteen. She studied at the Royal Academy of Music in London and also at the Banff Summer School in Canada. She has worked as principal oboist with the BBC Philharmonic and with the Royal Liverpool, Bournemouth, and Ulster Orchestras. In her charming Scottish accent, she provided most of the spoken commentary for this trio in this and other concerts.

She made a big hit in this program by playing "Danza Gaya" by her teacher, Madeline Dring, and later performed "Reel" by Skinner, arranged for her by her father, also a musician.

Katy had dark hair, white skin, and wore long, single-fabric dark dresses over her curvy body that magically swayed like a larger, more flexible oboe when she played.

The violinist in the trio was a tall, willowy, young man, Emil Chitakov, from Bulgaria, where he began his studies. He continued his studies at the Royal College of Music in London and at the Guildhall School of Music. He studied with violinists Schlomo Mintz, Igor Oistrach, and the Takasz Quartet.

He has performed with the London Schubert Players Chamber Orchestra since 1995, and has performed in Switzerland, Germany, France, Greece, Israel, and Belgium. He was also the violinist in the Quodlibed String Quartet which won the Carmel, California, Music Competition in 2000.

I always enjoyed watching Emil play, especially when he would swing into a gypsy czardas. The rapt expression on his face and the choreography of his body summoned up roaring campfires and good times. True to form, Brahms' "Hungarian Dance" was on the program, and the final item this evening was "Czardas" by Monti, both of which Emil played with particular relish.

The interesting personal aspect here is that Emil and Katy were engaged to be married, so that after they finished their work on board ship, they flew back to London to become man and wife.

These three young musicians, for me, were a cultural highlight of life aboard the QE2. It made me feel good about young people and the future of good music, something it is hard to experience in the raucous, noisy world we exist in these days.

These three fine musicians were brought to the ship under the auspices of the Concordia Theatre Company which also presented many other interesting musical programs, such as the piano recitals of Yitkin Seow, a Singapore native, who studied in England, beginning at age twelve, and at nineteen won the BBC Piano Competition. In 1977 he won the Arthur Rubinstein Prize. He has appeared at Carnegie Hall in New York and with the St. Petersburg, Russia, Philharmonic. We have had the pleasure of hearing Yitkin play on two voyages. He is a quiet, modest young man. I have especially enjoyed his Debussy, Schumann, and his much-admired Brahms' "Paganini Variations."

Welsh soprano Gillian Humphreys is the Artistic Director of Concordia, and, in addition to her singing, she is a striking beauty and fascinating woman in her own right. With her head of red hair and her stunning evening gowns, Gillian was a stand-out wherever she went on the QE2.

Born in Wales, she studied at the Royal Academy of Music in London and was a principal soprano with the D'Oyly Carte Opera Company. She has performed in theatre, opera, television, and radio, and founded Concordia to build bridges through music and the arts. A major current project of hers took place in June 2000 when her production of *Cavalleria Rusticana,* combining European and Vietnamese performers, opened the newly renovated opera house in Saigon, now called Ho Chi Minh City. Gillian's big hope on this voyage was that singers and musicians from the Ho Chi Minh Opera House would be able to perform on the QE2 one evening for the passengers.

This never came to pass, however. The musicians were stranded on the pier in Vung Tau, along with the passengers, and the sea was too rough that night to bring them out to the ship and back.

UP HILL AND DOWN DALE AT THE OPERA

Sometime back in 1993 or so when Rudd and I were at a cocktail party on board the Cunard *Princess* in the Aegean Sea approaching the Dardenelles, a man we were talking with said that we hadn't seen anything until we sailed into the harbor of Sydney, Australia, which, he swore, was superior to Hong Kong, Rio de Janeiro, or New York. I remembered that as the QE2 approached Sydney on our first visit in 1997.

What strikes one most about Sydney from the ship is its dramatic opera house. It looks like a great ship with many white sails. Situated at the end of Bennelong Point, it juts out well into the harbor, so that it is surrounded by water on three sides.

It looks great from the harbor and it is interesting to see on land and to walk up to, but then it changes dramatically from being an interesting sight to becoming an insurmountable object that you are expected to walk up hundreds of steps to enter. In this respect, it is reminiscent of many things back in London—the underground, for instance, with all those up-hill and down-dale steps that leave one huffing and puffing, and English flats, like the one we lived in in 1998 on Cromwell Road in South Kensington, five flights up, no lift, start hiking, good for the character, turns you into a sturdy Brit on the spot.

In 1997, Rudd and I saw a superb production of Strauss' *Die Fledermaus* in this lauded Sydney Opera House, our seats perfectly located sixth row center orchestra (stalls to Brits).

In 2001, we again went to the opera house, this time to see Emmerich Kalman's *Die Csardasfurstin* (*The Gypsy Princess*), sung in English. This 1915 operetta, although well done, was terribly dated. It presented a world of wine, women, and song, promoting the idea that love is everywhere and that people should forget their cares and follow a hedonistic philosophy.

This time we sat up in the balcony which we reached only after following an usher who led us to a freight elevator that ascended to the lobby entrance, From there, we had to walk up four long flights to our seats. When we decided to go to the restrooms before the program began, that necessitated going down a different flight of stairs and hiking back up again. Thoroughly winded, we finally collapsed high up in seventh heaven and tried our best to succumb to Kalman's musical charm.

So, once again, what we have in the Sydney Opera House is an architect's dream come true, but, typically, an impractical venue for anyone not in top physical condition. All that concrete and glass and gorgeous harbor views are nice on a starry night, but this vaunted palace is really a very cold, forbidding, remote building, almost as bad as the new Getty Museum in Los Angeles, located on an alp in Brentwood that you have to take a special mountain train to get to.

In Sydney's case, the story gets even more interesting. The designer was a Dane named Jorn Utzon who planned it in 1959. But there was so much controversy and delay, as there almost always is in municipal projects, that the building did not get completed until 1973, when costs rose above the projected 7 million dollars to 102 million.

Utzon walked out on the project in 1966, leaving Australian architects to complete it, and I am told that, to this day, Utzon has never seen his completed building that tourists and critics praise so highly. The idea of a building with sails positioned on a long peninsula in the harbor is a wonderful idea, of course, but, as I have indicated, you have to be something of a real rock climber to love it.

The other striking aspect of Sydney's harbor is the Sydney Harbor Bridge, opened in 1932, which stretches from Dawes Point to Milson's Point. It is one long arch, familiarly called "The Coathanger," because it looks like one. True to form, adventurous Aussies and foolhardy tourists actually pay to walk up the arch, and you can see them, peering down at the world from their dangerous perch high up.

Apart from these unusual objects, Sydney is full of skyscrapers, parks, handsome shopping streets and malls, quaint sections like The Rocks (The old historic section), the Royal Botanic Gardens, Darling Harbor, Chinatown, Kings Cross, Victoria Barracks, and Paddington, plus there are extensive suburbs. Altogether the population of Sydney is over three million, the largest and most cosmopolitan city in Australia.

Unfortunately, sometimes Sydney seems not to have gotten over its beginning as a penal colony in 1788. Aussies are fond of saying that Sydney always tries so hard to prove itself, as though trying to get over its past.

I found the pace of life very fast and sophisticated in this city. In 1997, we stayed at the Ritz Carlton Hotel for a few days before returning to the United States, but in 2001, although the hotel was still there, it is now called Sir Stamford Hotel. It is right across from the Royal Botanic Gardens, which was fine for me, and it enabled my wife and me to walk to many places, including the animated, bustling Circular Quay (Brits pronounce it "kee") and the Opera House out on the point.

Sydney's beaches are famous, and one day we went out to Bondi (pronounced BOND-eye) Beach, supposed to be good for surfing. It has a nice crescent-shaped beach, but the waves were small, so naturally there were few surfers around. The buildings were typically oceanside stuff, I felt, rather tacky, in fact, reminiscent of Asbury Park or Coney Island. No big deal here; no bodacious beach babes either.

In 2001, we took a rivercat out to Paramatta to see where the Olympic Village had been in Homebush Bay. The river trip was interesting, especially because the river kept getting smaller and narrower. I was surprised at all the highrises in Paramatta. The Olympic Village itself we could only see at a distance from the river as a few arcs cutting against the sky.

One afternoon we went shopping at the Queen Victoria Mall, an upscale boutique place housed in a former block-long Victorian vegetable market. I bought a custom-made shirt from designer Joe Banaras, who has designed for Tom Cruise, Shirley MacLaine, and other celebrities. He is part Chinese, part Australian, from Adelaide originally.

After three days in Sydney, we sailed on a Friday night and received quite a send-off. Many people and boats appeared, including a replica of H.M. S. Bounty under sail. I took more photos than I should have of the effect of sunset on the Opera House and Sydney itself.

But never underestimate the effort involved in climbing all those steps just to hear *La Traviata* for the hundreth time!

E-Mail from Verna Rudd Kenvin, Cabin no. 4127
To: Brooke, Heather
Date: Thursday, February 8

Hello again! Here we are sitting in Sydney harbor with a beautiful full moon coming up over the Opera House. The view is right out our porthole. We have been so lucky with the weather here—blue, blue sky, cool to warm, but not hot. No rain. Not like last time.

We did get tickets to the Opera, way up in the top balcony. The place has only one elevator in the Stage Door area, which handicapped people have to use. We took it up to the entrance to the Opera House because going up all those stairs is not easy on my bad leg. After that, it was four long flights of stairs, plus a stairway down to the Ladies' Room, and then back up two flights again. It was terrible, going down all that distance on the stairs, some without railings, and my vertigo kicking in.

We were able to walk along the quay (key) back to the ship with the moon shining brightly. A beautiful evening. The operetta was "The Gypsy Princess," not the best story, but well done. We had to have tea beforehand on the ship and then a midnight buffet afterward, since the performance started at 7:30 p.m. . . .

. . . P bought a gorgeous shirt today from the designer of jackets for Tom Cruise, Whoopi Goldberg, etc. Expensive, but beautiful. The Cruise-Kidman situation is big news out here since they have a home in Sydney.

Love again,

Mom

ON THE BANKS OF THE YARRA FAR AWAY

In 1997, I was up on deck at 6:00 a.m. watching our approach to Melbourne. We sailed through a long, fairly shallow bay—Phillips Bay. Melbourne seemed distant, stretched along the bay, the central part of the city looking a little like a head-on shot of New York from the Hudson—a cluster of skyscrapers in the central portion.

It was uncomfortably hot and humid there that Saturday, but the whole town turned out to greet us. Scottish pipers, kilted players, a town crier—a koala bear and a kangaroo, plus many people. All day long, throngs of people showed up on the pier and on the ship, among them Bill Unwin, brother of our English friend, Francis Unwin, who, with his wife, Eugenie, is now living in Brussels. Bill had lunch with us aboard the ship.

Saturday morning, we toured the city. Both guides had hard-to-understand Australian accents. We saw the university, the hospital, many parks and gardens, lots of charming galleried architecture, called by the Aussies "terraced apartments."

We went to Fitzroy Gardens to inspect Captain Cook's cottage, imported there from North Yorkshire, England, and then we went into the Conservatory at Carlton Gardens where the 1880 Great Exhibition was held. Next, we carefully went through Como House, a mid-nineteenth-century home with original furnishings—and some massive pine pieces from Tasmania. This was of particular interest to Rudd, who was a docent at Carlyle House in Alexandria, Virginia, for many years.

Toorak Village with its happy mix of restaurants, shops, and flats is considered very chic. Bill Unwin lives there. Toorak reminded me of New York's Greenwich Village and Jane Jacobs' urban philosophy of a nice mix of shops, homes, galleries, and markets.

Traveling along the quay, we went down colorful Fitzroy Street to St. Kilda where we found the beach and sailboats, always popular in Australian port cities.

Then, our departure Saturday evening was both memorable and touching, partly because it had been two years since the QE2 had last docked at Melbourne. The pier was jammed with throngs of people waving, a band playing "Auld Lang Syne," many boats accompanying us all the way out into the night. I've never seen such a tremendous send-off nor felt such a powerful surge of love directed toward a ship and its passengers and crew.

In 2001, we had two full days in Melbourne. This time, Bill, who had suffered a stroke, asked us to meet him for dinner at a restaurant in town. We met at Walter's Wine Bar, a trendy restaurant overlooking the Yarra River, which courses through the city. Bill's son, Peter, and wife, Sue, joined us. Peter was born in Capetown and Bill's daughter, Valerie, in Shanghai.

Bill has traveled extensively, but revealed that he always goes back to Yorkshire when he reaches England. His brother, Francis, on the other hand, is loyal to Belgium, because he was trapped there during World War II and lived with a Belgium family.

The next day, our friend from Hampshire, England, Cicely Campkin, came to lunch aboard the ship with her sister, Joan Williams, and their niece, Emily. Cicely and Emily were in Melbourne visiting Joan, who needs a wheelchair to get around these days. We obtained one from the hospital aboard the QE2 for her.

At midnight the ship sailed, and again a surprisingly large number of Melburnians turned out for the departure, attesting to the power of the QE2 as a sacred British symbol.

Melbourne's population is just under three million, but the look and feel of the city is different from Sydney's. Melbourne seems like a very graceful, comfortable nineteenth-century city. I had an impression of long, tree-lined boulevards, many beautiful parks, lots of theatres, libraries, art galleries—in other words, a city of culture, learning, and art.

Another aspect I liked was Melbourne's extensive inner-city tram system, giving it some of the quaintness you might associate with San Francisco or London. The people, too, seemed less pressured than those in Sydney. Maybe Melbourne is more European, or British, and Sydney, more like Hong Kong or New York—fast-paced.

One word of caution: It was extremely hot and humid in the city, and Melburnians will warn you of their large mosquitoes. In fact, I was amazed how buggy it is throughout Australia and of the varieties of rodents, reptiles, and insects found in the country. It would give me pause before settling there. And then there are all those sharks in the ocean!

The Royal Botanical Gardens on 88 acres in the King's Domain, a huge park, are justly world-famous for their varied collection of plants. Also very big in

Melbourne are football, tennis, horse racing and cricket. There are large stadiums for football and tennis and two large cricket grounds on the banks of the Yarra. The Melbourne Cup horse race is world famous.

Melbourne also reminded me somewhat of Buenos Aires in Argentina. It is a large cosmopolitan city with a European feel to it, very clearly a cultural focal point for local people and others who come great distances to view its museums, libraries, universities, sports venues, and art galleries. Melburnians also like to point out that their ancestors came there voluntarily. Sydney, take note!

ON SHIPBOARD

"Went to hear Mrs. Turner's daughter play on the harpsichon; but, Lord! it was enough to make any man sick to hear her; yet was I forced to commend her highly."

Samuel Pepys

This afternoon I went into the Grand Lounge on the QE2 to watch the passengers' amateur hour. The host was Cruise Director Colin Parker, an Oxford-educated Englishman with a deadpan face, an extremely dry, quick wit, and the patience of the Queen herself. Here is what I saw:

An ancient woman with ringlets of golden hair, an Alice-blue ballgown falling off her shoulder, a dowager's hump throwing her off center, creeps up to the microphone, clutching a basket of fake flowers, announces she is Mimi in Puccini's *La Boheme* and croaks out "Mi Chiamamo Mimi" like the ghost of Bette Davis in *Whatever Happened to Baby Jane*.

A short, stocky man from Florida mounts the stage, announces he recently saw Cole Porter's *Kiss Me, Kate* on Broadway "where tickets go for $250 a head" and belts out hoarsely "So in Love" in which his voice progressively descends from a quarter below the note to one half to a full tone below and the song chromatically slides down to its soggy death. "Strange, dear, but true, dear . . . "

Three Japanese ladies appear in beautiful traditional kimonos. Two sing their nasal song while the third gyrates in a timid dance. The incongruity of steel spectacles and an obi down below like a loose caboose doesn't bother her at all.

A six-feet four hulking man, looking like Lon Chaney as Frankenstein's monster, takes center stage, and, in stentorian tones, recites poems by Shelley and Byron, informing us that Lord Byron wrote "She Walks in Beauty like the Night" for Georgina Nathan, the daughter of his publisher.

A chipper young woman from South Carolina wearing a hat and gardening slacks good-humoredly waves her fan and recites Noel Coward's satirical "Mad Dogs and Englishmen Go Out in the Midday Sun," prompting an Englishwoman to say to me later, "Why does that woman dislike the English so much?" Colin, the Master of Ceremonies, simply said, "Just think. She came all the way here from Southern California to read that to us." I thought his substitution of California for Carolina was pretty funny.

A ninety-one year old tubby Australian woman wearing a flowered frock sang in an authoritative, commanding voice Bloody Mary's "Bali Hai" from *South Pacific* so convincingly that I would have cast her in that role on the spot. Goofy Colin said he thought he had made a mistake when he announced that she would sing that song, but the lady said, "Well, Colin, when people see me they often think they've made a mistake."

FIRE ON THE MOUNTAIN

With a total area of about 190 miles by 180 miles, Tasmania is roughly the size of Ireland. Interesting that Hobart is the hometown of a famous Irish-Australian film actor, Errol Flynn.

There are 450,000 inhabitants in Tasmania, of whom about one-third live in the capital city of Hobart.

Tasmania is named after a Dutch navigator, Abel Tasman, who landed on the island in 1642 and named it Van Diemen's Land in honor of the Governor-General of the Dutch East Indies. It was not called Tasmania until 1855, and in 1901 it was named one of Australia's six states, along with New South Wales, Victoria, Queensland, South Australia, and Western Australia, not to forget the two territories, Capital Territory, which surrounds Australia's official capital, Canberra, and the Northern Territories of which the capital is Darwin. Like Sydney in New South Wales, Tasmania from the beginning was used by the British as a dumping ground for prisoners. One of Tasmania's tourist attractions today is the old prison at Port Arthur.

We were not planning to visit any prisons, preferring instead to go up Mount Wellington, but Hobart had been in a very dry condition before we arrived and we found a full-fledged forest fire flaming on top of the mountain, so we went up Mount Nelson instead, and overlooked the city of Hobart with its harbor far below. The harbor is very deep and extensive and there are rolling hills, up to 4,000 feet high around it. Many of the houses are built on hills and the houses are attractive. Hobart looks clean and prosperous.

As one might expect of an island country, there are many boats there. Island people are always good sailors. Luckily for us, there was a three-day wooden boat regatta going on while we were in town, and so the port was full of lots of visitors day and night.

I was able to roam about and take many photos of all the activities. In the waterfront area, I discovered a bar called "Drunken Admiral Saloon" and an antique shop called "Mother Wouldn't Like It," indicative, probably, of a widespread appreciation of humor. I also took photos from Mount Rozny and the summit of Mount Nelson, as well as in the unusually fascinating Royal Botanic Gardens.

Our guide here was an informative, good-humored Melbourne native named Ian who had just retired to Hobart. It looked like a perfect place to retire. One could purchase an attractive home for much less than it would cost in Melbourne or Sydney, and, if one still wanted adventure in one's life, Hobart is a prime port from which to sail to Antarctica.

E-Mail from Verna Rudd Kenvin, Cabin no. 4127
To: Rob, Brooke, Heather
Date: Tuesday, February 13

We are getting ready to sail at midnight from Melbourne to Adelaide. We didn't take any tours here since we have been here before. But, last night, we took a cab to the center of town to have dinner with Bill Unwin, the brother of our former neighbor in Arlington, Virginia.

It was a lovely restaurant overlooking the Yarra River which runs through the middle of town. A superb meal, the best I have had in a long while, the last probably having been at that nice Silks place on the way from Boston up to New Hampshire. It was hot and humid, but we dined on the balcony and a bit of breeze helped. Then the wind changed suddenly, and it started to sprinkle. Fortunately, we got back to the ship before the downpour started.

Today, it is cloudy, but cool. We had lunch on board with Cicely Campkin. We met her on this same route in 1997 and will see her again in Southampton, near where she lives in Hampshire. She arrived with her sister, who is in a wheelchair. (We put down a $50 deposit and obtained a wheelchair from the ship's hospital.) Also, Cicely and Joan's niece, Emily, came to lunch. A lovely, but hectic day. . . . I did the complete ship's tour for Emily. . . .

. . . We won't call again until Hong Kong. Our next time change tomorrow night is only for half an hour. Odd! I will let all of you know the hour at which we will call. (The man at the computer next to me is falling asleep. He plays solitaire on his computer.)

Melbourne has grown a lot since we were last here. Now, a great many people are lining the dock to see us sail away. It always puts a lump in my throat as we wave, say goodbye, the horn toots, and we pull away. It takes nearly four hours to reach the entrance to this port!

Our visit in Hobart, Tasmania was short, but good—a lovely island, but in the midst of a severe drought, much as in California, even to a forest fire possibly started by arsonists. In all these Australian cities, except Sydney, much of the architecture reminds me of India—very Victorian. . . .

Did we tell you that one woman actually lives on the QE2? When the ship is in drydock, she stays in a nearby hotel.

There are many different nationalities and languages floating around the ship, which make it interesting. And, now that we are heading into areas we have not visited before, the trip is really becoming fascinating. . . .

Lots of love to everyone. We miss being in closer contact by phone but love getting the E-mails.

Love,

Rudd

THE BEST LAID PLANS

Adelaide is a planned city in the state of South Australia. The idea of Englishman Edward Gibbon Wakefield was to found an Australian city for civilized men and women, not convicts.

The perfect site was decided on in 1836, with all the streets planned by Colonel William Light, the Surveyor General of South Australia at that time. He saw to it that there would be spacious boulevards, parks, squares, and tree plantings. It was named Adelaide in honor of King William IV's wife.

Serious-minded Englishpeople arrived to form the first inhabitants, followed by many Germans who settled inland and worked the orchards and vineyards. This gave rise to a now-thriving Australian wine industry. Also, miners discovered those beautiful dark blue opals so highly prized by jewelers and their patrons.

About one million people live in Adelaide, representing three-quarters of South Australia's population. Adelaide also boasts a modern, white Festival Centre, opened in 1973, but, every two years since 1960, a huge arts festival is held which brings in thousands of other visitors. The Festival Centre has a theatre with 2,000 seats for opera, ballet, and big musical events, another theatre for plays, as well as an experimental theatre called "The Space," and an outdoor amphitheatre for open air events. On its plaza, sculptures are displayed and there are also puppet shows and story hours for children.

Adelaide, despite its city plan, seems very spread out, hard for a first-time visitor to grasp. We drove up to Mount Lofty for a quick, hazy, windy view of the city far below. Then we went to Cleland Conservation Park, a spacious place where one sees red and blue kangaroos, some with their Joeys, Tasmanian devils, wallabies, Dingo dogs, and emus in a beautiful setting.

From Cleland Park, we drove back through the center of town via the suburbs and outskirts. The outskirts were especially interesting to me because they were very much done in western style, with many homes sporting colorful facades, giving them a frontier-like appearance. Some homes had fences made out of woodpieces held together with wire. They look picturesque, but actually are quick to burn should someone's cigarette brush against them.

Very visible are many full-grown Norfolk Island pines (*aurecaria*) growing quite tall in this city. Norfolk Island, another island off the coast of Australia, is the native home of this particular tree, usually seen in the United States as a feathery, frondy indoor house plant, slow-growing.

Incidental intelligence from Australia: Aussies do not tip, in their country or out of it! If they are forced into it, they do it grudgingly. They expect a job to be done properly.

FRONTIER MILLIONAIRES

In the morning to Perth, capital of Western Australia, population 1.5 million, most of whom live in Perth.

Western Australia boasts the famous Outback, the Sahara of Australia, and was the site of the gold rush back in 1882 when gold was discovered at Kalgoorlie and Coolgardie, bringing in a lot of settlers. Actually, Western Australia was always a difficult place in which to find work, so the British brought in convicts for eighteen years beginning in 1850.

Today, Perth is a very busy, energetic city, with lots of sunshine, good business, and a very youthful population. Half of the people are under 24 years old and a lot of them are hard-working and very wealthy.

In the city, we saw the University of Western Australia, parks, and the war memorial. We drove through Perth's expensive suburbs, very handsome indeed.

Kings Park, a domain of 1,000 acres, looks out on the Swan River, which winds through Perth. Many of the buildings in town are brand new, but there is a little tribute to Mother England called London Court, a collection of shops, built in 1937, done up in Tudor English style with leaded windows, lanterns, and woodbeam and stucco composition.

Fremantle is the port city. The natives call it "Freo" for short. It is a much smaller place and totally different in character. It looks like an inviting frontier town—low, outback buildings, brightly painted, some grill work in the architecture, giving it a mini-New Orleans ambience.

Sidelight: A woman on the bus asked Malcolm, our driver, if he would point out a criminal. Malcolm replied that there were a lot of light-fingered people in the government.

With Malcolm at the wheel, we drove down along the beach area, also, which was impressive. Miles of beautiful clean beaches and clear, blue water. Many swimmers, surfers, campers. It all looked very appealing and pleasurable, except for the possibility of sharks lurking below the blue water surface of all that beauty.

ON SHIPBOARD

On any voyage like this, there usually are celebrities on board that everyone talks about and that one meets or has some connection to or with somewhere along the line.

On the first ship I ever took, the original *Queen Elizabeth* back in March 1953 from New York to Southampton, Bing Crosby and his son, Lindsay, about to enter Williams College, were aboard, as well as orchestra leader, Paul Whiteman, Charles Boyer, and David Niven. I bumped into Crosby and Lindsay on the promenade deck and Crosby very kindly let me photograph him with his trademark hat and pipe.

In 1970 on the *Bergensfjord*, heading for Oslo from New York, Johnny Mercer, the lyricist, was on board, and our two young daughters wanted to meet him because they loved his catchy lyrics to "Accentuate the Positive." We knocked on the door to his stateroom, and, again, he chatted nicely with us and posed for a photograph. A friendly Georgia gentleman.

In 1984, on the QE2, we knew Hermione Gingold was on board, heading home to England to die, after suffering a stroke in America, but we never saw her. However, actor George Hamilton was on board with his son Ashley, and I stood in line with him at the gambling casino one night when we both were buying chips. He had his customary dark tan and wore a white dinner jacket which heightened the lustrous tan. Ashley, then about ten years old, waited patiently for his father.

Sometimes celebrities participate in discussions or perform aboard the ship. Othertimes, they are just travelers and seek to preserve their privacy.

In 1998 on the *Vistafjord*, making a long circle voyage in the Pacific on the trail of Paul Gauguin, we had both kinds aboard. One was actress Patricia Neal, scheduled to give a talk, and the other was actor Gene Hackman, traveling privately with his wife.

I first became aware of Patricia Neal, while I sat waiting on a bench in the Embarkation Center of the Port of Los Angeles. A man entered and wheeled a woman sitting in a wheelchair very close to my bench. I recognized that Katharine-Cornell-great-actress look immediately. With her dark brown hair brushed out, one eye wandering somewhat, counting the house, perhaps, and taking in the audience around her, who recognized her, who didn't, she had a star's presence, no doubt about that. When she spoke, her deep, strong, raspy voice immediately announced that she was a special person to be reckoned with.

Later, I discovered that she was on the same deck as we were. I bumped into her with her companion and, startled, said, "Hello," as though to an old friend. "Hello," she replied, smiling. "How are you?" After that I saw her in the Beauty Parlor, playing bingo in the ballroom, and watching the revue *Forbidden Broadway*. She nodded off during the Stephen Sondheim section, but came to and laughed at the Carol Channing spoof. At tea one day, singer Maureen McGovern, also a passenger-performer, came by and chatted with Neal about her (McGovern's) upcoming performance. "Well, I'll just have to stay up late another night," said Neal.

One morning Neal was featured as a lecturer on the topic "As I Am," based on her autobiography. She told of her birth in Kentucky, her childhood in Knoxville, Tennessee, her determination to become an actress, her education at Northwestern University where her teacher was Armina Marshall.

She roomed later with three struggling actresses in New York until she got the part of Olive in the Chicago company of *The Voice of the Turtle* with K.T. Stevens.

Her next big part was in Lillian Hellman's *Another Part of the Forest*, for which she won a Tony award. Then she received offers from Hollywood, accepted one from Warner Brothers where she remained for three years, making *John Loves Mary* and *The Hasty Heart* with Ronald Reagan.

Later, she made Ayn Rand's *The Fountainhead* with Gary Cooper with whom she had a four-year love affair, and *Hud* with Paul Newman for which she won an Academy Award as Best Actress.

She met her husband, English writer Roald Dahl, at a party at Lillian Hellman's on 82nd Street in Manhattan. She was seated next to him at dinner, but he totally ignored her. However, he called the next day to ask for a date. They were married for thirty years until he left her for a friend of hers.

Neal told us of three more serious tragedies in her life:

1) Her baby, Theo, was hit in his carriage by a taxi in New York as his nurse pushed the carriage off the curb into the street.

2) Her daughter, Olivia, had measles, developed encephalitis, and died.

3) At age 39, Patricia Neal herself had a crippling stroke which affected her whole life.

The audience gave her a standing ovation. I talked with her afterward about her Warner Brothers' years and asked if she had worked with our friend, art director, John Beckman. She hadn't, but she had worked with director Michael Curtiz, one of Beckman's colleagues.

Gene Hackman, on the other hand, was very guarded. He was traveling with his wife, and both were terribly seasick, so that they terminated the voyage in Honolulu and flew back to their home in Santa Fe.

But when we docked in Aitutaki, Cook Island, on Thursday, March 19, 1998, Hackman and his wife sat with my wife and me on the tender going from the QE2 to the port and we chatted politely, as passengers do. When we got to the port, the four of us struck out, walking in the same direction, when suddenly we were hit with an unexpected monsoon-like downpour of rain.

I decided to head up to the postoffice to buy some stamps and so parted company. "Where are you going?" shouted out Hackman to me. "To the post office to get some stamps," I replied. He and his wife continued on through the rain to God knows where, while my wife and I sought shelter in the postoffice.

The Hackmans sat at a table not far from where we sat in the dining room, but because of their seasickness, they missed a number of dinners which, of course, they could take in their stateroom. The ship's television, meanwhile, was showing his film *The French Connection* in German, because there was a large German contingent among the passengers. A woman sitting at the table next to Hackman leaned over to him one lunchtime and said, "I loved hearing you speak German on television today." She reported that Hackman turned his back to her and never spoke to her again.

Othertimes, celebrities can be very cordial. When we sailed once on the *Delta Queen* on the Mississippi River, we discovered that Civil War authority Shelby Foote had the stateroom across from ours. He was on board as a paid lecturer and talked about various places such as Vicksburg and Natchez, as we visited them along the way.

In Greenville, Mississippi, where Foote was born, we walked into town with him, and again, got caught in a driving rain. "Should we get a cab back to the ship?" he asked. Since we wanted to make some long-distance calls, we demurred.

Later, after we had returned, changed and rested, I saw Foote come in, drenched, and all night long I heard him coughing in his cabin. But his commentaries were excellent and we enjoyed his company and commentary on board.

In 1994, we were on the *Sagafjord* off the coast of Brazil waiting for a total eclipse of the sun. Astronaut Buzz Aldrin was supposed to be on board, but we heard that he had had visa problems and couldn't get out of Brazil.

On board the ship, Hugh Downs and the *20/20* crew were waiting to photograph the whole event for television. The eclipse itself and the ship's ceremony around it were indeed impressive, what with world-famous astronomers aboard and hundreds of telescopes and cameras, plus three opera singers, and the ship's orchestra ready to belt out Beethoven's "Ode to Joy" at the right moment.

Another time, on the QE2, returning from England to New York, actor Roddy McDowell was on board, his last trip ever, since he died of brain cancer a few months later. I saw him around the ship a lot, went through the breakfast line with him once in the Lido, and he and Mariette Hartley performed A. R.

Gurney's *Love Letters* for the passengers. I also noticed McDowell photographing Gordon Davidson during his talk in the Grand Lounge. McDowell was an accomplished celebrity photographer.

One celebrity Rudd and I particularly enjoyed was Thomas Hoving, former Director of the Metropolitan Museum of Art in New York. We were entertained by his Robin Hood-like tales of art escapades. Hoving was a kind of Peck's Bad Boy of the Art World for a while, but he is a disarming speaker and a delightful person. We chatted briefly in our favorite bar, The Chart Room, one night, and I told him if he ever came to our house for dinner, I would certainly have to count the silverware after he left. He laughed, probably because he knew everybody else would say the same thing about him.

Another celebrity on that trip was Sheridan Morley, the son of English actor Robert Morley, and the grandson of actress Gladys Cooper. A writer and critic, Sheridan was a superb raconteur with his stories of people he had met in show business, but none of his stories were better than the ones about Robert and Gladys.

My two favorites both involved Gladys who had been an extraordinary beauty as well as a gifted actress in the English theatre. She was one of those, like Charles Laughton, Ronald Colman, Leslie Howard, and Basil Rathbone, that the movies paid high salaries to in the 1930s if they would only come and be their wonderful English selves in movie roles. Sheridan said Robert was always being cast as a conservative, reliable, English banker-gentleman type, even though in real life he was quite liberal in politics and loved horseracing passionately.

At any rate, Gladys Cooper became a leading hostess of the English colony in exile in Beverly Hills and she became famous for her Sunday afternoon

English teas on her lawn. She had been under contract at M.G.M. when somebody told Gladys that Louis B. Mayer, the head of the studio, was quite disappointed that she had never once invited him to her home.

She decided to make amends and issued an invitation to Mayer for a Sunday afternoon. David Niven was standing on the lawn chatting with another English actor when a huge black limousine pulled up and out stepped this tiny man, barely over five feet. "Good God," said Niven to his friend. "There's an American on Gladys' lawn."

The other story about Gladys is that she and Sheridan decided to drive across the United States one time and just stop whenever they felt like it at places along the way.

They pulled into one place where there was a Holiday Inn and both decided to have dinner there. Sheridan, who went ahead, reported that the dining room was reserved for a large General Motors convention staying there and that they couldn't be admitted. Gladys said, "Wait here," and disappeared into the motel.

When she came back, she said they had a table. "What happened?" asked Sheridan.

"I just told them I was an old friend of General Motors and that he would want us to have dinner here," Gladys replied.

"But, Gladys, darling," Sheridan replied. "General Motors is not a person. It's a corporation. It makes cars."

"Nonsense," said Gladys. "General Motors distinguished himself greatly in World War II. Now let's go in."

Another of Sheridan's stories concerned southern actress Tallulah Bankhead. It seems that an old romantic beau of hers came up to her in later life and asked, "Tallulah, don't you remember me? We were lovers forty years ago."

"Yes, darling," replied Tallulah, "but I thought I asked you to wait in the car."

Sheridan Morley and his wife, Ruth Leon, were not only on the QE2 then, but also on the 2001 voyage, as was singer Maureen McGovern whom we had seen before on the *Vistafjord*, and Christopher Dillon, another American singer we liked, whom we've encountered twice at sea.

A celebrity we both very much admired on the 2001 World Cruise was mystery writer Mary Higgins Clark. We had lunch with her and husband John, plus delightful Irish priest Father Nee, in the Lido one afternoon.

Mary and John had just renewed their wedding vows aboard the ship with Father Nee officiating. Mary was on board to deliver two lectures and then was to fly back from Southampton to New York to do the *Today Show* and after that on to Los Angeles for a book festival at U.C.L.A.

Some of Mary's very readable books are *A Stranger is Watching*, *Loves Music, Loves to Dance*, *Before I Say Goodbye*, and *We'll Meet Again*. We found out that, like us, she had lived in Stuyvesant Town in Manhattan, and had, in fact, raised four children there. Now she was redoing an old Victorian house in New Jersey and experiencing typical problems with contractors,

Her editor at Simon & Schuster, Michael Korda, who has worked with her for 24 years, went to Le Rosey School in Switzerland, where both Rudd and I had taught, although Korda was there the year before we arrived.

We found Mary's Irishness infectious. She is a good-humored, candid person, a great speaker and human being. She told funny stories on herself, of how one woman rushed up to her and said, "Mary Higgins Clark, my favorite writer of junk literature." Another said, "I always read your books before I go to bed. I usually fall asleep by page two." Her husband, John, too, was a pleasure to talk with. He knew Charles Merrill's grandson, also a former Le Rosey student.

Of course, it's not just celebrities that one remembers on cruises; it often is staff members, crew, and other passengers who make a good impression. My wife has been sailing on the Cunard Line since 1949 and I since 1953. Other lines we've been on include the Seabourn Line, the French Line, the Holland-America Line, Norwegian Line, and the Delta Line. We remember captains, staff, crew, waiters, and passengers, and it is always fun to renew acquaintances with them.

On this world cruise, a particular favorite was our waiter, Merwyn, from a 1999 voyage, now kicked upstairs to the Queen's Grill, probably because of his excellent work. Merwyn's good news is that he and his fiancée would be getting married in Bombay, now Mumbai, in December, 2001. Merwyn, Warren, and company were part of what they called "The Bombay Mafia," who enlivened our dining room hours on the QE2 and always looked after us with the greatest of care.

Royal Palace, Amlapura, Bali

A PRINCELY RECEPTION IN AMLAPURA

"But hearing oftentimes
The still, sad music of humanity."

William Wordsworth

Bali was a big surprise to me, and not really a pleasant one. I guess I had allowed popular impressions to seep into my mind, so that I was thinking too much of "Bali Hai" from *South Pacific*, an idyllic, small island full of pleasant, carefree people boating, swimming, and singing all day. A dream of a desert island where anybody would love to escape to forever.

Paradoxically, I had already visited the Society Islands in French Polynesia where Bora Bora, Moorea, and Tahiti all fitted this romantic image, except for the ring of broken glass and plastic bottles that litters their shores everywhere. But listen to what I found in Bali.

We landed at Padangbai, a port where the Dutch first arrived in 1597. From my porthole I could see the enormous volcano, 10,000 feet tall Mount Agung, looming up over what looked like a giant rain forest. I knew the volcano had last erupted in 1963 and that the residents down below had to live very circumspectly because of it, as people do in certain parts of Hawaii, Italy, and Sicily.

We had to go into the port in tenders. The people had set up shops in low buildings on the pier, but none of us was prepared for the aggressive onslaught of young kids hawking souvenirs and shouting out "One dollar." It was so severe that one could not move freely. My wife fled back to the ship when the tender headed out to sea again, as did others, and the Cunard officials had to reprimand the crowd, even physically restraining them in some instances. It was not a very welcoming greeting.

I pushed through the crowd, photographing and walking purposefully to try to see something. A young woman thrust wooden beads into my pants' pocket and hung another strand of beads around my shoulder. I handed back one strand, but gave her a dollar to get her out of my way. She still pursued me. Looking up, I saw what was distinctly a Muslim shop and entered, hoping I could shake her. It worked.

Why it worked is that I knew Bali was 90% Hindu. But what I did not know in advance is that Bali's population is 3 million inhabitants on an island that is 50 miles wide by 87 miles long, so that it is much bigger, much noisier and more crowded, and the distances greater, than one can imagine.

Bali, actually, is only a small part of an enormous nation. Indonesia's total population is almost 225 million spread out over 13,500 islands covering a distance of 741,000 square miles. That is vast by any standards. The capital city is Jakarta which has over 11 million inhabitants.

Two wars were even raging while we were there—one in Molucca between Muslims and Christians with casualties of 2,500 since January 1999 and the other in East Timor, which Indonesia captured in 1976, and where 200,000 Timorese have died as a result. So the island of Bali looks pretty tame by contrast.

The Hindu religion is a rarity in most of Indonesia. Indonesia's inhabitants are predominantly Muslim, so that Bali is quite distinctive in this large country. Naturally, because of its Hinduism, it reminded me more of India than any other place.

Hinduism came to the island originally prior to the 11th century from Java, but in the 15th and 16th centuries Java gradually became more Muslim, leaving Bali to develop its own kind of Hindu-Dharma religion, which is a mixture of Hinduism and Buddhism. One notices that, in the architecture all over Bali, individual homes have little shrines in their outside yards to which citizens make offerings every day of food and flowers.

This appears to be a major preoccupation of almost all Balinese—spirit houses to worship their ancestors, and ominipresent temples for the gods. There are over 20,000 Hindu temples on the island. Religion, obviously, is a major part of most people's lives here.

Geographically, the island is a kind of large rainforest, confirming my first impression, and there is plenty of water. The Balinese have developed an ingenious method of farming, using rice terraces on the mountainsides, which give the otherwise wild-looking geography a carefully cultivated look in places.

However, the dampness means that everything rots sooner or later, so that one is aware that all life and objects here appear to be part of the cycle of growth and decay. One remembers that Hindus believe in rebirth, so that one understands how all this is consonant with their overall philosophy. The Balinese are friendly and courteous, as a result. They smile a lot and are charming to talk with, that is, unless they are trying to sell you something.

We visited Tenganan Village, quite an interesting old town, built on a slope, where there were lots of shops with artisans and artists inviting one in to look at their work and handicrafts, carved wooden objects, jewelry, masks, paper scrolls—much of the material religious in nature, typically, depictions of Shiva, Ganesh, and scenes from the *Ramayana*.

One shop I visited had musical instruments for sale, the kind used in the Balinese and Javanese gamelan orchestras, tinkling, clanging, xylophonic sounds like jangling temple bells, casting a reassuring spell on one. But other shops had young people hawking postcards, cheaply crafted wooden chess sets, bowls, vases, animal sculptures.

Later, we went to the town of Amlapura where we visited the Royal Palace, which was a compound with a number of buildings, including a temple, a central courtyard, and a nicely landscaped pond with a temple on an island and a bridge out to it. A luncheon was prepared for us, a gamelan orchestra played, and some beautiful Balinese women danced.

The handsome young prince addressed us in English. Both before his speech and after, I talked with him and his wife. He was twenty-six years old, slim, shy, and his wife held their two-year old child. They were very gracious to me and other visitors from the ship.

In the royal compound I photographed some small children playing under the banyan trees, a Balinese girl in a traditional costume, the prince and his family, and some of the buildings I saw.

People seem to live harmoniously in groups and social interaction is ongoing. In fact, the Balinese sense of community stems from the way their villages are organized, and this, apparently, is true of other parts of Indonesia. Each village is made up of smaller groups, all tied together in a covenant of cooperation, so that one has to request permission from the village authorities even to move to another village.

This makes gregariousness the normal pattern of life. The Balinese do not like nor really understand Westerners' desire for solitude or time alone. This seems like a bad idea to them. Demons could possess one at such times.

The Balinese see the world as held in a balancing act between good and evil. This is not unlike the quietism found in India, especially in the Hindu religion, a quite beautiful philosophy that formed the basis of Mohandas Gandhi's thinking.

Often, as we traveled around the island, I thought of the different layers of civilization in Bali—the Dutch who held sway over the Balinese until after World War II, the Japanese who conquered Indonesia during World War II, the 1965 military coup which put General Suharto into power and then his dismissal in 1998.

The gentle people of Bali have suffered the same tyrannies that some other small countries have—the injustices of the strong and powerful over the meek.

ON SHIPBOARD

Conversation overheard on the quarter deck outside the ship's library:

I was sitting in a chair waiting for the library and neighboring bookstore to open when I tuned into the conversation of two men talking close by. One was a big, hearty American, who was questioning a quieter, more reserved Englishman.

Ordinarily, I probably would have blotted something like this out of my mind and concentrated even more deeply on what I was reading, but the American man's questions seemed intelligent, informed, and cogent, so that I looked up briefly to see the source of this interrogation, and then, back again at my book, hoping they would continue. They did and bits of what they said slipped in and out of focus.

Apparently the British man was originally a Scotsman with a name something like James Innus (which he pronounced as "Ingus") Angus Matthew MacGregor, followed by a surname that was apparently Norwegian. He told the American he had three children, all named after cowboys—Rory, Dale, and Gary.

He then was questioned by the American about his progenitors, and so began talking about his grandfather, who, he said, had been turned out of an orphanage at age thirteen, given only a crown for money, and told to make his way on his own.

The enterprising young man then got a room and began doing prize fights, getting beaten up to make more money.

After that, he became a painter. He painted a piano for a bar and then began painting pictures in other bars. As a result, he gained a reputation as a master painter and decorator.

Gradually he built up a thriving, prosperous business. Now his grandson, James Innus Angus Matthew MacGregor something Norwegian has a big empire in Newcastle-on-Tyne to which he added contracting and building, plus all three of his children as executives.

This unfolding Dickensian novel gave me great pause in what I was reading and made my morning wait a sheer delight.

Sometimes you do meet really interesting people with great stories to tell on board ship. But I wish I had that inquisitive American guy with me always to run interference. Whenever I saw him in the future, I would always gravitate to a place near him in the hope he would open up another winning oyster of a conversation.

But it never happened again.

E-Mail from Verna Rudd Kenvin, Cabin no. 4127
To: Brooke, Heather, Rob
Date: Thursday, February 22

Hello again, to all. In about 50 minutes we pull up anchor and set sail for Manila. We have been here off Bali for 2 days. The first day we had no tour, so we thought we would just take the launch over to the mainland—a 25 minute trip. I was having a great deal of vertigo. It's no fun getting into the launch with everything bobbing up and down as you are trying to step in, but, happily, there are many strong men willing to give me help.

Once on land, however, I was hopeless, as I had forgotten to bring along my cane, and many people descended on all the passengers, pestering people to buy this or that. Roger went off to look at some shops, but I turned around to take the next launch back, having purchased the postcards we wanted—$1 for 6 cards, although the next person offered 10 for $1. Such is Bali!

Our tour today was much of the same. As we drove out to an old palace for a dance show, I just kept being reminded of India. Mildewed buildings, people sitting around with nothing to do, small buildings in poor repair, people going to temples with offerings (This is mainly a Hindu country), and children dressed rather raggedly. This country is not a place to enjoy, in my estimation. The Aussies love it because it is closer to Perth than Sydney, and cheap—$400 a week for a place to stay. But the hot, humid climate is there all year and so are the very persistent sellers, whose wares, to me, do not really seem well made. I am glad we came this once, though, so I will not have to succumb to those people who say, "Oh, you really just have to go to Bali!"

Perth, however, was a really pleasant surprise. It has rolling hills and a lovely river winding through it. Neat houses on small plots, but well kept up. Even the more expensive homes are, in general, on relatively small plots of land. . . . Perth's port, Fremantle, was quaint, and newly spruced up, thanks to the Americas' Cup having been held there a few years ago. Because of our five stops in Australia, we have had a lot of Aussies on board going to either Bali or Hong Kong. Many got off today. I hope we will have fewer on board for a while.

We have seen a few good movies on the tv, attended several good concerts, and saw the very first episodes of *Upstairs, Downstairs*, which we had missed back home. So life is quite busy, no matter what. We also were invited to a cocktail party where we met some new, delightful people—one, an Englishman, whose brothers, like him, use their middle names, as I do. I also met Beatrice Muller, the woman whose home is the QE2, and, yesterday, we met a passenger who graduated from Sarah Lawrence College in 1943—Ruth Meyer Epstein. She also goes to Maine near Orr's Island, but her permanent home is Bronxville.

Glad to hear that Brooke met Lois, Marion, and her children at Mary Ann's house in North Hollywood. Papa did send Lois the very first card from Hawaii and another which he mailed yesterday from Bali . . . . Hope Joan is doing well. . . .

Love,

Rudd

MACARTHUR PARK

"We are left, finally, to decide why
the world goes, and we with it,
toward some strange kind of return."

William Virgil Davis

I knew we were headed for disappointment in Manila when our two regular waiters on board ship flatly refused to disembark when the ship docked in port. "I've been there before," said one. "I can't stand wall-to-wall garbage. I don't want to touch all that filth."

As we sailed into Manila Bay, I began to see what he meant. Debris and trash of all sorts floated on the water. It looked like the dumping ground of the Pacific, and it would continue even after we left Manila and headed north to Japan. An Australian yachtsman standing next to me in the stern of the ship said with disdain, "Look at that. It's disgusting. It affects us in Australia, too."

Others on board the QE2 confided to me, "The only reason we stop here is to take on new crew and let others off. That's why we stay for two days."

I observed many of the Filippino crew trudging down the corridors with their luggage, some of them having been at sea for a long time.

I was told that a Filippino waiter on the QE2 could make the same salary as a bank president in Manila. A Filippino guide later told me that the Philippines' greatest export was nurses to the United States, and then I remembered many of the very good Filippino nurses who had helped me in various hospitals in America.

Estimates of the number of people in the capital city vary. Our Manila guide said 14 million; others said around or over 10 million. The total population for the Philippines is a little more than 81 million located on 7,100 islands in an area of 1,100 miles.

Manila is located on the big island of Luzon with its wide crescent-shaped harbor framing famous Manila Bay. The city has an old section called Intramuros, dating from the 16th century, many new post-World War II skyscrapers mimicking New York's, and a new park-like arts complex, largely thanks to the efforts of Imelda Marcos, the shoe-loving widow of Dictator Fernando Marcos. Like Eva Peron in Argentina, Imelda is probably a mixture of the good and the imperial. Imelda's contribution, called the Cultural Center Complex, provides conference rooms, concerts, films, and other arts in large Soviet-like concrete buildings on land which was reclaimed from the sea, since Manila itself is so heavily congested and built up.

Basic to an understanding of present-day Manila is the fact that Manila was the second most heavily bombed city in World War II, second only to Warsaw, Poland. Much of the city is relatively new and hastily built up. It looks unfinished in many places.

The other fact one needs to know is that in the Philippines 10% of the rich people control 40% of all the wealth; 55% of the people are poor; and the rest, about 35%, are middle class.

As we traveled throughout the city, I saw all these layers of relative prosperity and poverty. The numbers of people, the traffic congestion, the pollution were enormous.

Manilans admitted the Bay was polluted, but when I asked why were people swimming in it, the reply was that only the poor swim in it, the rich have swimming pools, and the others go outside the city limits.

We visited the grand Manila Hotel with its elegant champagne glass dining room. General Douglas MacArthur and his family lived on the top floor. I wondered how anyone could take any meal in this beautiful hotel in good conscience, considering the stark contrasts outside.

Perhaps the true center of Manila is Rizal Park, named in honor of Dr. José Rizal, a leader, writer, scientist, and artist, who is a national hero, with a distinctive statue of him in the park. He was shot by a Spanish firing squad in 1896.

We also drove through Forbes Park with its lavish mansions and went through Makati, an upscale business and recreational area. I was impressed with the high quality of Filippino products available in an official folk arts emporium.

The Philippines' history is also responsible for another aspect of its life today. It is the only predominantly Roman Catholic country in all Asia.

Again, like some of the other Asian countries we had already been to, the indigenous people from Malaysia, Borneo, and Sumatra who emigrated to the the Philippine islands over 30,000 years ago were subjected to a number of invaders, all of whom left their indelible marks. First came the Arabs in the 14th century bringing the Muslim religion with them. Then in 1521 Ferdinand Magellan arrived and claimed the land for Spain. To press their point, in 1571 the

Spanish knocked down the old Muslim town and set up a Spanish rule, sending in Catholic friars to convert the people to Catholicism.

In 1763, the British defeated the Spanish in the Seven Years' War, but the Treaty of Paris returned Manila to Spain. However, in the Spanish-American War of 1898, the United States seized control of the Philippines and imposed their rule on it until 1935 when they granted it some autonomy.

In 1942, the Japanese invaders struck and occupied Manila, forcing General Douglas MacArthur to issue his "I shall return" speech, which he kept, winning Manila back in 1945.

On its feet again, the Philippines elected Ferdinand Marcos president in 1965, but he proved dictatorial and was deposed in 1986. Since then the Philippines has had Corazon Aquino (1986), General Fidel Ramos (1992) and Joseph Estrada (1998) who, like Ronald Reagan, is a former movie star.

The most beautiful sight I saw in Manila was a serene place high up on a hill overlooking the city. The 150-acre park is called The American Cemetery in Manila, and in this tranquil, well-landscaped park lie the remains of 17,206 American armed forces, some with their names inscribed on the walls, others in grassy plots marked by gleaming white stone crosses. I wandered among these tombstones for quite a while, reading the inscriptions, thinking about the waste of war, the avarice of nations, and the immorality of conquests, such as I have described above.

Ultimately, my feelings are mixed about Manila and huge cities in general. Manila, with its searing poverty and polluted wars, seems a lot like Rio de Janeiro. How can one enjoy its geographical beauty when so many people live in the trough of desperation every day of their lives?

The biggest event in the lives of many of the people I encountered in Manila was the recent visit of the current Pope, John Paul II. Over three million people turned out to greet their religious leader. What message, aside from "Keep the faith" did he bring to his flock? Bali with its Hinduism, Manila with its Catholicism. Both with so much poverty and its concomitant lack of quality of life.

What price, salvation now?

E-Mail from Verna Rudd Kenvin, Cabin no. 4127
To: Brooke, Heather, Rob
Date: Tuesday, February 27

. . . We had a very interesting visit to Manila. It was Sunday, so there was not much traffic and we were able to see more of the city than expected. Still, what traffic there was was crazy—going through red lights, turning left from right hand lanes—Yikes! A very interesting city, though, but much poverty, many shanties next to modern office buildings and 5-star hotels. The old Manila Hotel, where General MacArthur lived, was fabulous. The War Memorial and the American Cemetery were very moving. The city and country have survived so many problems—wars, invasions, earthquakes, horrendous bombing.

At the cemetery there were mosaic maps of the various battles. We are passing through that area now—Corregidor, Mindenao, Bataan. It really reminds you of how large an area was involved.

By the time we reach Kobe, it will have been eight days since Fremantle. The ship has been averaging around 20 knots per hour. The Manila stop is done mainly for crew turnover, since many of the crew are from the Philippines, including our cabin steward, Rolando. Nurses are the Philippines' leading export, as David and Brooke well know.

P and I agree we would not want to do this long a trip again, although many on board have and continue to do so. But it is a wonderful way to really experience the size of the world and see the differences in the varied cultures. As our friend in India, Miss Padmabai Rubgundi, used to say, "People are very different all over the world." I would also add to that that you can really see the damage organized religions have done to so many people. . . .

Love to all,

Rudd

Kasuga Taisha Shrine, Nara, Japan

"I RISE IN ASHES CRIES THE PHOENIX"

"I find it impossible, however, to accept such a thing as a past which has not yet begun."

Kobo Abe

March 1, 2001: We arrived at Kobe, a large port city of 1.5 million people and received the most enthusiastic welcome of our entire voyage. Helicopters circled overhead, fireboats came out and shot up pink, yellow, green, and blue fountains off our starboard bow. People lined the port building waving to us.

What we found was an amazing city with hospitable people, all the more remarkable because in 1995 Kobe suffered a violent earthquake which killed 6,400 people and caused heavy destruction of buildings. But you would not know it to look at Kobe today. The industrious citizens went right to work repairing the damage so that you would have to look hard and long to see any traces of it. Kobe has been remarkably restored.

Kobe was also almost completely obliterated in World War II by American bombs. It is a tribute to the resilience and enterprise of the Japanese that they snap back so expertly.

Mostly what I saw of Kobe was the vast port area, the tall skyscrapers, the bridges, and fast thoroughfares. We were aiming on this trip for a smaller, more beautiful town called Nara.

We zoomed through Kobe and the neighboring industrial city of Osaka, passed through a long tunnel 7 kilometers long and emerged into Nara.

There is a long tradition of Buddhism that began in Nara in the 8th century and still exists today. Nara Park is the central attraction with hundreds of deer that roam freely. We were also properly impressed by the enormous and strikingly beautiful Todaji Temple, the world's largest wooden building, which houses the world's largest bronze Buddha (53 feet tall), as well as other Buddhist icons, both inside and outside the temple.

Many schoolchildren were there while we visited. When I photographed them, they all made the Churchillian V-for victory sign with their fingers, which I thought was interesting. Odd that this relic of World War II should have survived in this fashion to be used for British and American visitors.

After Todaji, we went to the Kasuga Taisha Shrine, a Shintoist shrine painted bright orange-red, boasting thousands of hanging lanterns and dating back to the year 768. It was the Shintoist religion that had to be broken after World War II because the religion held that the Emperor Hirohito was divine, and so that fanaticism fueled the behavior of the Japanese warriors in action. Destroying that concept was a major task of General Douglas MacArthur.

Japan's history reveals that the country traditionally has had problems adjusting to the world around it. Its long love-hate relationship with China, for instance, has led to endless invasions. Japan's attitude toward trade has sometimes been intransigent, and the idea of a divine emperor drove it into World War II aggression and an unholy alliance with Nazi Germany.

But now, modern Japan seems to have recovered handsomely and has resumed its place as a productive, attractive country. Compared to Indonesia and the Philippines, the Japanese archipelago occupies only 145,882 square miles, primarily on four islands that are extremely subject to violent earthquakes. The overall population is nearly 127 million.

Emperor Akihito heads what is now a parliamentary democracy. As everyone knows, Japan is also a mighty industrial producer, especially in electrical and electronic equipment.

One saw the new Japan at the Nara Hotel where we had lunch. Businessmen in expensive cars and tailored suits dined all around us, discussing business just as executives do in New York, London, Paris, and Hong Kong. One saw almost no evidence of poverty in the whole area.

And the send-off the residents of Kobe gave us when we departed was enormous and touching. They sent off fireworks into the night. People stood out in the cold on the pier, singing "Auld Lang Syne" to us while the band played. It was the expression of a people who were very pleased to have a ship with visitors from other lands in their harbor.

I thought of the previous time I had been in Japan back in 1965. I came with my wife and two small daughters in an airplane. We went first to Tokyo.

I had requested an authentic Japanese Inn rather than one of the highrise hotels, and finally one was located in a central area. I had to carry a card on which was written the address because in those streets the numbers went according to date the buildings were constructed, which meant that #1 could be in the middle of the block, #2 might be at the opposite end, and #3 right in the middle, on the opposite side of the street.

My usual practice of freely walking through a city had to be modified also, because my unfamiliarity with the Japanese language meant that I could not read signs as I went along and did not know what they conveyed.

I became dependent on taxicabs and friends like Paul and Agnes Fukashima who were a great help in getting us around to Asakusa Park and me to Kanze Kaikan theatre and the Kabuki-Za Theatre.

I have never seen such heavy traffic on the roads, such honking of horns and kamikaze driving as in Tokyo. How the ordinary citizens manage, I do not know. This extends even to their splendid subway system which teems with people, and where they have special persons whose job is to take their feet and push more people into the cars like sardines into a can.

We took a train out of Tokyo and went up to Hakone to the charming resort of Miyanoshita where we stayed at the beautiful inn there. We also saw Mount Fuji, floating in the distance, elegant and serene, certainly the most beautiful mountain I have ever seen, exactly like a perfectly arranged Japanese woodcut. At Miyanoshita I indulged in the luxury of the Japanese baths, so relaxing and soothing. I respond easily to Japanese architecture and lifestyle, which spoils one in a very pleasant way.

Also from Tokyo, we took a train down to Kyoto, which, like Nara, is one of Japan's most gorgeous cities, now swollen to almost 1.5 million people. On the return, we took the famous super-fast train.

I like to call Kyoto the Athens of Japan. It was once the capital of all Japan and for hundreds of years also the residence of the emperors. Kyoto, indeed, is so full of artistic treasures that it was not bombed by the Allies in World War II. It is one of the most magnificent cities of the entire world.

Again, we stayed at an authentic Japanese Inn, the Tarawa, and saw the major sights, including Nijo Castle, dating from the 17th century, surrounded by a moat with swans. Nijo Castle has unusual "Nightingale floors" that squeak when one walks on them, thus warning residents of possible intruders by night.

We also saw the Heian Shrine, reproducing on a small scale Kyoto's first imperial palace, built in 798, and surrounded by beautiful iris gardens and cherry trees, and Kinkaku-ji, called the Golden Pavilion, which is a replica of the one dating from 1397 which burned down in 1950.

My favorite place, however, was Ryoanji, where there is a stone garden with carefully raked small white pebbles in a large area, looking like a sea with jagged mountains (the fifteen large rocks) in it. We were invited to sit there and meditate for a few minutes. We were all startled when four-year old Heather blurted out, "It was like being born again." Was there something she experienced that we had not?

Art mingles well with nature in Kyoto. Along with Venice, Italy, Kyoto is a unique city that one long remembers and wishes to return to.

E-Mail from Verna Rudd Kenvin, Cabin no. 4127
To: Brooke, Heather, Rob
Date: Friday, March 2

Yesterday we had a wonderful, but very tiring trip to Nara, Japan, where we saw the largest bronze Buddha statue in the largest wooden building. The Buddha was built in 800 A.D. Six people can stand on one of its hands.

The wooden building housing this Buddha is the third one. The previous two burned down. The area around the temple is very interesting, with many deer roaming around freely. They like food and paper, so that when I went to blow my nose and pulled out some kleenex from my pocketbook, the deer grabbed part of it from my hand. I had to be more careful after that.

We had an excellent guide who, after we had visited a Shinto shrine, told us that 80% of the Japanese are followers of both Buddhism and the Shinto religion. Roger explained that one is good for this world, and the other for the next world. Hedging your religions, I call it.

We docked in Kobe's huge harbor during the morning. The city had an earthquake in 1995 that killed 6,400 people and demolished many places. It has now been rebuilt and many people have returned. They do not use the old architecture much because it is too expensive to make it fireproof, so the current architecture is rather dull. But the old places, such as in Nara and Kyoto, are still lovely. The Japanese have a knack for harmonizing landscape and buildings. . . .

The shopping in Japan was zilch. What was available near the pier was expensive and poorly made. We are told the pierside shops and the mall nearby in Hong Kong are great. Hope we can get things there. We have three days . . . .

Lots of love to all,

Rudd

FRAGRANT HARBOR

"He who neglects to drink of the spring of experience is likely to die of thirst in the desert of ignorance."

Ling Po

March 4, 5, 6, 2001: The QE2 docked at Hong Kong, the legendary city whose very name is a jaunty poem.

Many changes since we were last here in 1965, not the least that the city is now officially part of the People's Republic of China. There are more tall buildings, cold shafts of steel and glass thrust against the mountains and sky, overly-crowded together, creating a vertical, cluttered look against a beautiful background and a natural harbor. However, old Hong Kong always had that tall, gawky slum appearance anyway. Today the city seems cleaner. I saw many street cleaners and sweepers out in force keeping the place in order.

Perhaps this cleanliness has come about since Hong Kong reverted to China. It was a Crown Colony of Great Britain from 1842 until 1997. The agreement now is that China will allow Hong Kong to keep its capitalistic system for fifty years. It is and has been an international center for banks and trade, and enjoys a prosperity different from that on mainland China.

Actually, Hong Kong is another collection of islands, plus a chunk of the mainland. Hong Kong Island is its center and the other large island is Lantau Island. The two major pieces of the mainland are Kowloon and the New Territories which abut

Guangdong Province in China itself. The geographical area is 422 square miles, housing a population of about 7.12 million, of whom about 20,000 are British subjects. Through Hong Kong, also, passed many refugees from China, many of them on their way to the United States and Canada where they have now settled.

On the first day, we went up once again to the top of Victoria Peak (1,800 feet) for a panoramic view of the city and harbor. Many people were up there since it was Sunday. Later, we went to Stanley Market via Repulse Bay and Deepwater Bay where wealthy Hong Kong residents have built their splendid homes and keep their yachts, and then to Aberdeen Harbor, which may be the largest floating market in the world. Some people live on sanpans or junks year round. We toured the harbor in sanpans (each boat holds only twelve people) and saw, among other things, the Jumbo Restaurant, a huge, brightly-painted floating restaurant.

On the sanpans, the captains are usually women, who do this while their husbands are out fishing. The captain of the sanpan I was on was a really bossy woman, ordering people about, shouting out commands in Chinese. We called her "Captain Bligh."

The next morning, my wife and I had an elegant breakfast at the posh Peninsula Hotel, owned by a former student of ours at Le Rosey School in Switzerland, Michael Kadoorie, whose family business supplies energy to Hong Kong and Shanghai. They also own all the Peninsula Hotels, plus Michael runs a helicopter service in Hong Kong. He very kindly invited us to dinner with his family in their Deepwater Bay home. We had a great time there, meeting his wife Betty, her mother Berthe (who lives in Miami), and Michael and Betty's children, Natalie (15), Bettina

THE SIEGE OF VUNG TAU

March 8, 9, 2001: We docked at Vung Tau, on the southern tip of Viet Nam in the South China Sea, and took the bus up to Saigon, now called Ho Chi Minh City, and the hydrofoil back down the Saigon River.

Our guide was Phuc, pronounced "Foo." One of thirteen children, ten girls, three boys, Phuc explained that the oldest son in the family had most of the responsibility. Phuc is a university student, studying history and also Russian. He said older Vietnamese might know French, but not the younger ones. Phuc said he wanted to go to Russia to continue his studies. He was a Buddhist, like some 70% of the Vietnamese. The rest are Roman Catholics and other denominations.

Phuc took us to the Reunification Palace, and then to lunch at the Equatorial Hotel, and, following that, to the History Museum where we saw an imaginative puppet show with puppets in the water.

We also drove through Chinatown to the main square to see the Rex Hotel, Opera House, Government Building, Post Office, Catholic Cathedral of Notre Dame, etc. Very crowded, busy city. People on mopeds; nobody stops. It is dangerous to cross the streets.

In the suburbs one notices slums, as in India, people living in hovels, shacks, poverty, shops in front right on the street. Rice fields in background.

On the return, we waited on the pier four hours before we were able to board the tenders that took us back to the QE2. We sat on the concrete pier enduring all this waiting stoically until punchiness set in and people began acting foolishly.

We watched the pink sunset and the bright, full moon rise. In the silver shivers of moonlight, I wondered about these frivolous people, like us, who sign up for world cruises. I was convinced that we all had been born under a Magellan moon that infected us with a traveling madness that made us want to circumnavigate the globe.

The trip on the tender back to the ship was so rough that it didn't seem as though we were re-boarding the ship; it seemed more like a rescue at sea.

Vung Tau used to be called Cap St. Jacques when the country was under French domination. People from Saigon used to go there for relaxing week-ends by the sea.

Actually, Vietnam is one of those long narrow countries stretching about 1,000 miles north and south, but only about 30 miles wide at its thickest and boasting 2,000 miles of coastline. There are mountains as high as 10,000 feet, but most Vietnamese live along two rivers, the Red River in the north and the Mekong River in the south. The country is bordered by China, Cambodia, Laos and the South China Sea, which is where we waited patiently for our tender back to the QE2 in what I call the Siege of Vung Tau.

I thought about the history of Vietnam and felt ambivalent about the United States' involvement in the recent war there. In its early, very ancient years, Vietnam came under China's domination beginning in the second century A.D. In the eleventh century A.D. Vietnam became independent and recognized by China, but it had to defeat the infamous Kublai Khan and his army in 1288.

There were other political and military problems for the country along the way, but the next serious problem came from the French who did not like the unwelcome reception given its Christian missionaries, so they invaded Saigon in 1859 and soon took over the whole country which they called Indochine.

In the twentieth-century, Ho Chi Minh set up the Indochina Communist Party in 1930, but during World War II the country was invaded by the Japanese who received cooperation from the Vichy French government. The result was further opposition on the part of the Vietnamese people and the Viet Minh guerilla movement sprang up.

As is well known, the French army was finally defeated at Dien Bien Phu in 1954, after which a cease-fire was effected between Ho Chi Minh and the Communists in the north and Ngo Dinh Diem, an autocrat, in the south.

The United States of America backed Diem who lost power in a political coup in 1963, after which the United States dropped bombs and sent over 500,000 troops in a hotly contested war where the Viet Cong guerillas, as they had done in the past, stealthily defended their land from foreign invaders.

After the 1968 Tet offensive by the Viet Cong and, coupled with strong protests from many Americans, the United States finally withdrew, but in 1975 the North Vietnamese invaded the south and reunified the country under Communist rule in 1976.

Saigon is now called Ho Chi Minh City, the Communists have opened up the country to tourists, and one of the main attractions in Ho Chi Minh City is the War Crimes Museum where one can view the atrocities committed by Vietnam's enemies, most notably the United States.

Today, Ho Chi Minh City is a city of about 4 million people. It has leafy, tree-lined streets, low buildings always, people on bicycles, mopeds, lots of bustle and activity.

The large, brick Catholic Cathedral of Notre Dame sits near the center, very nineteenth-century and high-and-mighty, with its twin Romanesque towers, and solid presence, reminding one that many Vietnamese, perhaps as many as 30%, are Catholic. I wondered if this did not partly motivate France and America, the God-is-on-our-side Brigade, against the innocent Buddhist inhabitants in that reprehensible war.

Downtown Ho Chi Minh City also has some tall buildings and hotels that we all saw on television when the war was reported. The Rex, for instance, from the top of which the television newspeople broadcast their commentaries, and the Caravelle, a center for the war correspondents.

Cholon is the Chinese section. We visited a Buddhist temple there in which monks held up pyramidal coils which are ignited and send up smoke signals through the roof, little messages from the faithful to the dead on high. There were also huge terra cotta pots filled with sand into which people placed smoking joss sticks.

Cholon borders on the Saigon River from which thousands of Vietnamese boat people risked their lives to escape the horrors of war in the 1970s. The river is quite wide and choppy at the point where we boarded a hydrofoil for the long trip back down the Saigon River to Vung Tau.

My visit to Viet Nam saddened me a lot because of the recent war. The Vietnamese that I met and saw were friendly and peaceful and did not deserve the kind of treatment they received from outside invaders during the war. When I next look at the Vietnamese wall in Washington D.C, which I have stood before many times, I will include the Vietnamese in my thoughts, as well as the Americans who fell, and I will remember how the United States and French governments betrayed their own ethics to try to conquer some good people in a small country.

In Ho Chi Minh City, after I came out of the Museum of History, an old woman suddenly appeared before me, holding out her Vietnamese ricefield hat, called a *non la* for money. I gave her a dollar bill, a small token for a large injustice.

We had lunch at the Equatorial Hotel, a large yellow and white building with a bronze statue of a man and woman in front raising their arms. I wondered if this was a symbol of reunification of North and South Vietnam or merely the north and south portions of the world around the equator, given the hotel's significant name.

A major sight in Ho Chi Minh City is the Reunification Hall, which, formerly, was the official palace of the French governor. It dates from 1868 and is what you might call a mini-Versailles, large banquet halls, reception rooms, formal gardens, a huge circular lawn with vistas of the city beyond, a fountain not in use now, long banquet tables, artistic wall coverings, and ostentatious chandeliers, quite formal and offensively ruling-class French.

Reunification Hall stands now, a little aloof, now quite empty, not used, except to usher tourists through, as though the government cannot decide what purpose the building truly has in the new Vietnamese Communistic world. One thing I notice, though, is a formal Vietnamese garden, tiered up like a pagoda, in a courtyard. But the Reunification Hall ultimately fails on all counts: It must be an embarrassment to the current government, and, from a traveler's point of view, it is a glaring example of French colonial stupidity.

In the History Museum we saw a creative puppet show. We were ushered into a special, small theatre, pagoda style, with a toy lake between us in the amphitheatre and the curtained stage. Then a fish, a dragon, and ducks emerged from the water and began a water battle, followed by puppets representing men and women who also came up through the water and did their own particular choreographies.

At the end, the curtain was abruptly raised to reveal four men who had puppets on the end of long bamboo poles. They manipulated them from behind the scene and under the water. It was quite unusual and delightful, different from the Wayang Kulit puppetry of Thailand and the Bunraku of Japan.

I did not see any visible damage from the recent war in Vietnam, but then again, I was not looking for any. I don't doubt that there is plenty. I know in Cambodia, there are still dangerous land mines all over the countryside.

But the worst scars of war are those in the hearts of people who cannot forget.

E-Mail from Verna Rudd Kenvin, Cabin no. 4127
To: Bob Williams
Date: March 9

Dear Bob,

. . . Roger and I are not sure where you are right now,
but I think you said you can receive E-mail almost
anywhere . . . .

Brooke has E-mailed us about the problem
caused by our roof leaking into the dining room, but
she has been sick with the flu and unable to follow up
on it . . . . If you are in Arcadia at any time after a
rain, could you please check on the house, especially
in the upstairs bedroom near the sliding glass doors
and in the dining room to the left of the stairway and
give her a call?. . .

Our trip is going along very well. Our last stop
was Viet Nam. It was an anchor stop, which meant
that we had to use launches to get in and out. The sea
was very rough, so it made for some scary travel to
and from shore. Today's trips into port were canceled.
All other ports have been no problem, thank goodness,
and the weather has been very cooperative. . . .

Hope things are going well with you and that
you are in Arcadia to receive this E-mail. Roger sends
his best.

All the best,

Rudd

A PUZZLE THAI STYLE

March 11, 12, 2001:   We docked at Laem Chabang in the Gulf of Thailand and took a bus to Bangkok, passing through Pattaya on the way up. Pattaya is a flashy beach resort with palm trees, gin mills, all the water sports and a very active Thai night life. It is about ninety miles from Bangkok.

There is an elevated highway running practically all the way up from Pattaya to Bangkok. This was not here when we were last in Thailand in 1965. It reminded me of the Long Island Expressway running through Queens in New York City, especially since there are hundreds of new skyscrapers and apartment buildings in and surrounding Bangkok.

The city has spread both up and out. One notices tremendous contrasts as the bus flies along—slum areas, high rises, ancient Buddhist temples, all loom up in the landscape, and, of course, the motor traffic on the highway and in Bangkok has increased, also.

We took a boat trip on the Chao Phraya River and into some of the klongs off it, as we did in 1965, only this time our guide wanted to show us some of the grander, wealthier-looking homes, which we appreciated, even though they are far outnumbered by the hovels that most people live in.

The floating market is always fascinating, as is the number of open-air restaurants and the picture of canal life that one can see from the boat. At one place we stopped and were given loaves of bread to feed to the fish who whipped up a frenzy of feeding for our alleged pleasure. But, the new Bangkok seems to be overwhelming the old one, which is a shame, because it is the old Thailand, called "Siam" before 1939, that is most distinctive.

Old Bangkok includes the impressive Grand Palace with its looming monster statues warding off evil spirits outside its doors and the Wat Phra Kaeo, which is the royal chapel and Temple of the Emerald Buddha (really jade), whose costume is changed by the king himself. It was raining seriously this time, so, instead of going inside, as I had in 1965, I sat outside and photographed other people waiting patiently to enter the temple.

We saw again Wat Arun, the Temple of the Dawn, in its prime location on the river. This popular landmark is about as tall as a twenty storey skyscraper.

I also enjoyed the Royal Barge Museum, with its three huge, beautifully decorated barges used by the kings. Such sights remind one of the story of the English schoolteacher Anna Leonowens and the King of Siam, made into a book, play, and musical, *The King and I*. That king was King Mongkut, who took the name of Rama IV. His son, educated by Anna, became Rama V and he abolished slavery, endowed the national library, schools, and a museum, and established the first post office in Siam.

Oddly, Thailand aided the Allies against Germany in World War I, but in World War II it joined with the Axis powers, probably because it hoped Japan would return some stolen territory.

After the war, it joined the United Nations, and seems to have made a remarkable economic recovery, with one major setback in 1997. But it is now a tangled confusion of the old and new, with the modern winning out.

However, some things do not change so much. The beautiful Oriental Hotel still reigns along the waterfront. In 1965, we had an excellent lunch there, as we did this time, although the dining room is now arranged Japanese-style with low tables.

Also, in 1965 we went to an Institute of Thai dancing, where choreography of the finest sort was shown. This time the dancers came to us on the ship in the evening, and, although it was interesting, it was not as impressive as before.

Another curiosity: Our bus driver, who told us he had been born into poverty, was an ardent royalist. The Thais seem to like their current ruler, King Bhumibol Adulyadej, but it appears that only a small percentage of the over 61 million people in Thailand are rich, maybe ten to twelve percent are middle class, and all the rest are poor. That makes for a very unbalanced wealth distribution.

Bangkok, the capital, has a population estimated at a little more than 7 million. Thailand is situated on a peninsula along with neighbors Laos, Myanmar (Burma), Cambodia, and Malaysia. To get to another part of Thailand, we had to sail out and around, stopping at Singapore first. But to keep Thailand all together in this journal, I am going to jump now to the other side—Phuket—and record my impressions of our visit there.

PHUKET, THAILAND

Betty Kadoorie, our friend in Hong Kong, had recently returned from Phuket (pronounced poo-KET) and had praised this resort community, but warned us to beware of jellyfish in the water. She had been badly stung by one, which caused a violent itching rash on her leg.

Phuket Island, about thirty miles long and ten miles wide, has a population of about 200,000 residents. It ships tin ore, seafood, rubber, and wood, but is building a reputation as a top tourist destination because of its beaches and unusual limestone geography.

When the QE2 docked at Patong Beach, we took a tender into the shore and then a bus out to Phang Nga Bay where we were to take a lengthy boat trip to and around other islands in this fascinating Tolkien-like landscape of limestone mountains, caves, hidden beaches, and villages on stilts.

The curious outcroppings of mountains with their ziggurat and conical shapes looked grey-green and the waters of Phang Nga Bay were yellow-green. At one point, our boat shot right through a cave in an outcropping and we emerged on the other side, having passed right through a mountain.

We went to the fishing village of Ko Pannyi which is built on stilts with boardwalks throughout. The village was dominated by a mosque with blue roofs, so that one knew it had a predominantly Muslim population. The village originally was famous for its shrimp-fishing, but now many tourists visit, and so souvenir shops have sprung up also. I walked along, photographing some of the residents in their daily life.

Another unusual island we went to was Koh Khao Ping Gun, known as James Bond Island, because in 1974 the James Bond movie *The Man with the Golden Gun*, starring Roger Moore, was filmed there, and it has subsequently become a great tourist attraction. It features a towering, twisted peak, a sandy beach, and cavernous apertures.

On Phuket Island, we also visited Wat Tham Suwan Kuha, a Buddhist temple over two hundred years old actually located in a huge cave. The place was swarming with aggressive monkeys that made one feel uncomfortable. They swarmed all over the mountainside like so many large rats,

On the way back, we stopped at a Thai handicrafts center near Patong Beach where I bought four Thai silk neckties for relatives and two small painted elephants for our grandsons.

Back at the port, I saw people on the beach, in the water, on waterskis and paragliding, but I remembered Betty Kadoorie's warning, and so did not try the water myself.

ON SHIPBOARD

Observed in the Lido on the QE2:

A man wearing a T-shirt reading "The rain in Spain falls mainly in Seattle."

Flower market, Singapore

AT THE SIGN OF THE MERLION

"Too many boatmen will run the boat up to the top of a mountain"

Japanese proverb

March 15, 16, 2001: Singapore is an island republic off the tip of the Malay peninsula in Southeast Asia. It is about 250 square miles and its capital is Singapore City which houses 3.5 million of its over 4 million inhabitants.

Modern Singapore is unusual among its neighbors in that it is remarkably clean, law-abiding, literate (91%) and prosperous. It, like Hong Kong, is an international banking center.

The government, under current president, S.R. Nathan, enforces the laws strictly and also maintains a strong hold on political dissent. The city is extremely clean, modern, and impressive, if you like tall skyscrapers and the gentrification of areas formerly occupied by shop-houses along the boat quay on the Singapore River.

Not everybody does. A fellow American passenger on the QE2 stopped me as we were looking at architect Mies van der Rohe's skyscraper and, with a frown on his forehead, said, "Roger, this place has no spirit. It lacks soul." I asked him what he thought about Bali and he indicated he preferred that to Singapore.

Singapore, however, is animated, and I appreciated the fact that its citizens are among the greatest readers in the world. Library usage and bookstore buying statistics corroborate this.

The population is over 70% Chinese with Malaysians, Indians, and others. There are four languages—Malay, English, Mandarin Chinese, and Tamil. The religions, also, are diverse—Buddhism, Taoism, Islam, Hinduism, and Christianity.

On our first day in town we went out on bum boats (that is what they are called) on the Singapore River. We saw the colorful shop-houses, the gleaming skyscrapers, the bridges, the boats, the intriguing people, and the statues and sculptures along the riverfront.

One of these was the Merlion, a combination fish and lion. Apparently, Singapore means "lion city" although lions are not indigenous to the area and I don't think anyone ever saw a lion outside the zoo. Perhaps they confused it with tigers which once existed in the swampy jungles around.

Another interesting sculpture is a really plump bird, looking like an overfed robin, similar to the bird on Singapore's currency. This statue was erected to bring money and prosperity to the city, which it unquestionably has done.

A unique Singaporean sculpture is of a group of boys jumping over the sidewall into the river. This is so vivid and real that it always attracts attention.

We also went in individual rickshaws through the city's traffic to the famous Raffles Hotel, a glamorous, mysterious place that has figured in the writings of Rudyard Kipling, Joseph Conrad, and Somerset Maugham, among others. It opened in 1887 and its Long Bar with hundreds of ceiling fans is world-famous. We had Singapore Slings in this dark, woody, clubby bar where the drink was invented—gin, cherry heering, cointreau, benedictine, topped with a slice of fresh pineapple and a cherry.

The hotel got its name from the founder of Singapore, Sir Thomas Stamford Raffles, who founded a trading post on the island in 1819 and declared the island to be "a free port with trade open to ships of every nation."

Obviously, it worked, partly because the philosophy was right, and also because the harbor is huge. In the early years, tea and opium from China were leading products, as were tin and rubber. Now, banking and other business interests, plus tourism, have supplanted them.

Singapore's history has been relatively stable. From 1819 to 1959 it was a colony of Great Britain. In 1941 it was bombed by the Japanese and occupied by them from 1942 until 1945. It spent two years as part of the Federation of Malaysia, but then withdrew from that and became a completely independent republic in 1965.

On our second day in port, we went to visit the financial center of town, the Asian Arts Museum, a Hindu temple and a Buddhist temple located side by side in an orange and yellow flower market, as well as the National University of Singapore.

One can tell from what we visited how important the idea of money is to Singaporeans, but it should be pointed out that there is also a Chinese district, an Indian district, an upscale Orchard Road district, and even Singapore's own amusement park, Sentosa Island, over to which you can fly in a cable car, providing a panoramic view of the city and harbor. Plus the parks, gardens, trees all look verdant and well-tended, in a city about which the chief adjective used is often "immaculate," as in "clean," but maybe in Singapore's case, also as in "conception," meaning that Raffles had a good idea about free trade in a free port in the first place.

ON SHIPBOARD

Overheard conversation in the ship's theatre:

While I was sitting in the theatre waiting for a concert to begin, a tall, rangy Englishman in full tuxedo talked to two men sitting in front of me in the front row. All I could see was the black mane of the man to whom he was addressing most of his comments. The man seemed to be an American, judging from his speech.

Englishman: "Well, just where exactly are you from?"

Black-haired American: "Chicago."

Englishman (rocking back on his heels a bit): "Oh? I'm London."

E-Mail from Verna Rudd Kenvin, Cabin no. 4127
To: Heather and Tom, Norma and Lou, Joan and Rob,
Brooke and David
Date: March 15

Greetings, all! The first part is especially for Kyle.

Dear Kyle,

When we came back from our tour of Singapore
yesterday afternoon, we found a letter had been put
under our door. It was from you. What a nice letter
with hearts and good wishes. We are having a happy
voyage, but, at times, it is very tiring. Today it was
very hot and humid and we walked a lot. What nice
handwriting you have. Thank you so very much.

Love,

Gramma and Poppy

For Joan and Rob: I tried calling you yesterday, but
all you probably heard was a lot of strange noise. A
welcoming dragon dance was playing in the
background and your answering machine probably did
not pick up my voice. Sorry. Hope you had a good time
in New York. What about my sending a card to Ruth?

We have had two tours of Singapore. One
included a ride down the river in a bumboat, followed
by a ride in a trishaw—a bicycle with a sidecar for one
person. It was a bit harrowing as about 20 of us in our
own vehicles went careening through the traffic to the
Raffles Hotel where we had Singapore Slings at the

Long Bar. Singapore is a very attractive city. The skyscrapers are more spread out than Hong Kong, and the river front has been better preserved than Hong Kong's.

Today, our tour concentrated on the architecture and the influence of Feng Shui from Chinese beliefs. There are many parks along the highway, but our guide said the next time we visit the city, there will be highrises there. Apparently this park-like setting is merely landfill waiting to firm up before housing and office buildings can be put on it.

Since telephoning is so difficult from our port cities, I think we will not try to phone again until Naples, if we get there. There are rumors (ever present on board ship) that we have not yet been given permission to go through the Suez Canal. Thank goodness for E-mail.

I'm not sure if I wrote about our visit to Ho Chi Minh City in Viet Nam. It was a very interesting trip, but a long day which ended with a four hour wait before we could even get on the launch to take us back to the ship. Even then, the disembarkation from the launch to the QE2 was scary. The next day no one could go ashore because of the roughness of the ocean.

The tour to Bangkok was also very long. The city has grown considerably since we were there in 1965. Many more highrises, fewer canals, but still many temples and shrines, and many poor people still living along the klongs, but now they have city water coming into their houses, so that I did not see anyone brushing his teeth in the klong water as before. We had lunch at the same Oriental Hotel we ate at in 1965, but now the dining room is geared to Japanese tourists. One sits on the floor, a cushion at one's back, and tucks one's legs under the table—a difficult maneuver for me. And, after seeing all the open markets in town, I opted for a vegetarian lunch here. I travel mainly to see the geography of the area and the people, not to try the food.

I am beginning to feel that if this is Tuesday, it must be Hong Kong. I try to keep up in my journal, but I can only do it on the days at sea, and sometimes I am too tired to do it. Well, the memories are somewhere in my brain, and Roger is very good about taking photographs.

We sail back to Thailand on March 17th, the beach area around Phuket. Michael Kadoorie's wife had just been there. She said it was lovely.

Many of our new friends from the ship have left for home now. Singapore is a big departure point. More new faces to see tonight. Did we tell you Tommy Tune is aboard? He did a great show and will do another shortly. . . .

We did have a funny experience with our visas the other day when the Purser made it sound as though it was our fault for not having the proper visas for Viet Nam. But the Vietnamese will not issue visas ahead of time to those traveling by ship. Odd. . . .

Love to all,

Rudd

THE MEANING OF KITES

Sri Lanka, population 19,238,575 million, is a country slightly smaller than Ireland, and another island community. The people are predominantly Buddhist Sinhalese, then some Hindu Tamils, Muslims, and others. Its turbulent history includes invasion by the Portuguese (1505), the Dutch (1658), and finally the British (1796-1972) when it was known as Ceylon, but finally broke away to become The Democratic Socialist Republic of Sri Lanka.

Since the 1980s it has been plagued by a civil war between the Sinhalese and the Tamils, which was still raging in the north during our visit. This reflects some of the differences in its close neighbor to the north, India, where the Tamils of the south have frequently been culturally at odds with the Hindus of the north, partly because the Tamils have their own language and the New Delhi government has tried to impose Hindi as the official language.

This situation exists also in Sri Lanka.

It is not surprising, then, that the first thing I saw at 6:00 a.m. as I looked out the porthole was an ominous grey gunboat with guns mounted, sailing around the QE2. The container port where we docked was loaded with uniformed, armed soldiers and police, and I noticed that some of the guards were carrying machine guns.

When we boarded our bus to begin our tour of the capital city, Colombo, I saw that some of the streets around town were barricaded by soldiers carrying guns.

We saw the Sri Lanka History Museum, a large,

rambling, fairly dilapidated, old colonial building in a traditional garden setting. Inside were Buddhas, silver, crockery, and school children on excursions.

Later, we saw other government buildings, including one they called "The White House," the National University of Sri Lanka, the Library, and the Hilton Hotel, and we stopped to have refreshments at the Galle Face Hotel, a wonderful old Wuthering Heights of a British colonial hotel with frontage on the Indian Ocean and a great beach. Above the hotel I saw many kites fluttering in the sky, like so many white doves of peace. But in the city itself there was the tenseness of guns at the ready.

In the heart of Colombo I saw many poor people, garbage piled up, a not very happy-looking populace, mostly small, dark, Dravidians. I was able to coax smiles out of them and shy waves occasionally, and some of them tolerantly allowed me to photograph them.

It was excessively hot and humid, as one might expect, so that, after photographing, I returned early to the bus to enjoy the air-conditioning. Rudd returned with two beautiful kites for our grandsons, which we added to the two stamp and coin collections and small brass crocodiles and lions I had bought for them.

The heat and the limited access because of the military presence made Colombo a disappointing stop for me. Some people on the QE2 went on a journey up to an elephant farm in Kandy, but they did not fare much better, having had to deal with heat, bad roads, fast drivers, military blockages, for a short visit with elephants writhing in mud baths.

EXPLORING THE MALABAR CAVES

"Successive summers and monsoons had robbed the paints on the doors and windows and woodwork of their brightness and the walls of their original color, and had put in their place tints and shades of their own choice. And though the house had lost its resplendence, it had now a more human look."

R. K. Narayan

Today, March 22nd, was a day of anticipation since this would mark the first time Rudd and I have returned to India since we lived there in 1965-66. We each decided to do separate tours. Rudd wanted to visit Gandhi's house and see other in-town sights. I wanted to visit the caves on Elephanta Island which were fictionalized as the Malabar Caves in E. M. Forster's novel *A Passage to India*.

It took about an hour for the boat to make the six-mile trip out to Elephanta Island, the real name of which is Gharapuri, the home of about one thousand people, although the total population of Mumbai is about 13 million in an India which has about 900 million people and growing daily.

The unique aspect of the caves is that they are very old, dating from 630-635 A.D. They are dedicated to Shiva, who represents both creation and destruction, and the central item in the caves is a representation of the lingam (phallus) which here is a cylindrical stone on a square base. Followers worship it as the source of life.

The caves contain carved panels and statues of Shiva in various poses. Most notable is the huge 18 feet tall panel of the three-faced Shiva, revealing him as destroyer, creator, and complete god.

In E. M. Forster's novel, an elderly English-woman, Mrs. Moore, a younger English spinster, Adela Quested, and an Indian doctor, Dr. Aziz, enter the caves and, unnerved, perhaps, by all this eroticism, Miss Quested feels that someone has touched her. A trial later takes place with suspicion centering on Dr. Aziz. The psychological element in the novel is one of sexual hysteria, although English culture versus Indian culture is clearly the larger context.

To get to the caves, once you have landed on the island, you have to walk up over 100 steps or go up in a sedan chair, called a palanquin, which is a hard wooden cart supported on two poles, carried by four boys or men. I elected to try the sedan chair, which was bumpy, fast, and very hard on my back, so that, on the return, I chose to walk down instead, browsing at the vendors' many stalls along the way, most of them selling religious souvenirs of one sort or the other.

Outside the caves at the top were the usual band of monkeys, cute perhaps, but always dangerous because of their vicious biting ability.

The main cave is large, perhaps 130 feet square, and the entrance to it is marked by great pillars which look as though they are supporting the small mountain top above it into which the cave is cut.

Oddly, I realized that the group of people who entered with me and our female guide were very like some of E. M. Forster's characters. For instance, there was a tall, very stooped 91-year old woman, who came up the hill in her wheelchair inside one of the sedan chairs. She had tubes in her nose, and her tall son carried the oxygen tank she needed for her breathing.

At other times, he whipped out his camcorder and recorded everything around him.

Sometimes I would see his mother, breathlessly sitting down, sucking air. Other times, I would see her staring at a sculpture or straining to listen to the guide's explanation. People tended to part whenever she lurched into view. She certainly showed pluck and determination on this and other tours I saw her on. Once, she and her son sat directly in front of my wife and me on a bus in another country, and he rose up in his seat so much to record scenes through the window that I couldn't see much myself.

In the caves, there was more natural light than I imagined there would be, although that could be because the sculptures were artfully lighted by design. I was amazed at how varied and expertly executed the sculptures and panels were, although some of them had been damaged and mutilated. The guide several times and very pointedly said the carvings had been damaged by the Portuguese.

There were many Indians with their children going through the caves, as well as tourists from other parts of the world. The day was bright, clear, and not too hot, and the view from the entrance was very attractive.

On the way down, I bought two red Ganeshas for our grandsons and a double elephant carved out of stone for Rudd. A man came up alongside me wanting to talk and to find out where I came from, what I did for a living, how many children I had, etc., all those things Indians love to ask the first time they meet you. When he found out I had been a professor at a university, he was delighted because he, too, was a professor, and he insisted we exchange addresses with promises to write. "There will be many things we will be wanting to discuss in correspondence," he averred. I expected to find a letter waiting from him when I arrived back home in California, but it never came.

This brief return to India, however, made me feel good. I like the country and its people very much and want them always to succeed. Rudd, too, was pleased with her visit. She felt good about India again, also.

The only thing I cannot understand: Why on earth would you rename the city "Mumbai" when it was known by the distinctive, vivid name of "Bombay" from 1668 to 1996?

ON SHIPBOARD

MAD COCKTAIL PARTY ON THE ARABIAN SEA

"Natura il fece, e poi ruppe la stampa."

Ludovico Ariosto

The most glamorous occasions on the QE2 take place primarily in the Queen's Room on the quarterdeck. These would include the elegant teas every afternoon from 4:00 p.m. to 5:00 p.m. where the waiters and waitresses in white gloves and uniforms serve up sandwiches, scones, dessert and tea to passengers seated in armchairs and comfortable banquettes listening to live music, often a harpist or pianist playing classic Gershwin, Webber, Coward, or Rodgers tunes.

At night, the Queen's Room is the setting for dancers with the Wyn Davis orchestra playing at 8:45 p.m. and 10:30 p.m. plus vocalist Jon Fisher. On special occasions the whole room is transformed into a Hawaiian paradise, an Indian palace, a Balinese garden, an oasis in the Sahara for theme balls, for which the passengers dress accordingly.

Other times, the Queen's Room is taken over for occasions such as the captain's cocktail parties, the Cunard World Cruise Club parties, and formal ceremonies of the sort when the Sultan of Dubai came aboard, or the officials of Kobe, Japan.

The room is named after the current Queen Elizabeth, who is represented by a bronze bust in a niche at the end of the room. She casts a cautious eye on all activities from this central, yet discreet vantage point. Nothing escapes her gaze.

The armchairs are currently upholstered in either deep royal blue or gold. I always sit in a blue chair because they are high-backed and have side wings that screen out unwanted onlookers.

Into this setting on the evening of March 24th, we were invited to a formal World Cruise cocktail party for those who had in the past or were just now doing the complete world cruise.

We had gone through the lineup outside the room to greet our host, the captain, his officers and some of the staff, once again, and we were plunged into the room to find it laden with all kinds of special hors d'oeuvres and waiters briskly serving people who were settling in, or hugging and kissing one another, and hastily ordering drinks in almost the same breath.

Finding ourselves near the bust of the Queen and seeing my favorite high-backed chair empty, along with several others in a semicircle, I plunked down here. Rudd said she was going to look for a friend and case the hors d'oeuvres, so that left me all alone in my small fiefdom.

Suddenly, a bald-headed man, built like a bullet, a smaller version of Benito Mussolini, shot into the chair next to me. He nodded and said, *"Buonasera, signior."* I replied in Italian, but wondered how far I could go with this since I had only self-taught myself enough Italian to pass a reading exam for my Master's at Harvard back in 1956.

I saw immediately that Il Duce was suffering from the effects of a stroke since his hand shook when he put down his gin and tonic and he had to struggle to reach it again. I picked up his glass and handed it to him. Then he tried to pour out some niblets from the small-necked bottle they were in, so I took a cocktail napkin, spread it out, and poured some tidbits on it for his easier reach. He nodded *grazie* and indicated he wanted another gin and tonic. I hailed a waiter and placed the order for him.

Initially, a bit stand-offish, he now relaxed and began talking more volubly to me in Italian. I replied that I loved his language, but did he know French which would be much easier for me? He said a few words in French, but hopped right back into Italian again, while I responded in a melange of French, Italian, and probably Spanish too by this time.

The waiter brought him his new gin and tonic and he began interviewing me—where from? married? how many children? what did I do?

In response, I asked him the same questions, learned he was from Rome, told him I had taught the Borghese twins at school in Switzerland, loved the Hassler-Villa Medici, Passetto's Ristorante in the Piazza Navone—all those desperate straws you throw out when you know you are losing ground in a conversation.

A dark presence, like a Kafaesque wall, suddenly loomed up in front of us, and lowered itself heavily into the easy chair directly opposite Benito. I felt basilisk eyes burning into mine and recognized the person as a woman I often saw very early in the morning at the early birds' breakfast in the Pavilion in the stern of the ship. Shortly after, she could be found falling asleep in one of the ship's corridors outside the Grand Lounge, Queen's Room, or near the Chart Room Bar.

She now smiled simply, but said nothing to either Benito or me. I remembered then that someone had told me this woman was unpredictable, one day affable, another day uncommunicative.

Whatever her mood was this evening, she unleashed something in Benito's soul. He began talking to me excitedly in Italian, referring to Basiliska as being *"una ragazza brava"* among other things. I realized quickly that he was appraising her as one man to the other and that a rough translation of what he was saying amounted to "she's built like a brick shithouse, that one."

Basiliska, aware that the two men were talking about her, and now vastly interested, asked me in English, "What's he saying? What's he saying?"

As translator, I thought to soften the blow: "He says you are a very lovely person."

That worked all too well. Basiliska began to slide forward in a downward slouch toward Benito and spread her legs wider.

Inspired, Benito said she was *"simpatico"* and ordered another gin and tonic.

"What's he saying? What's he's saying?"

"He says you are a very sympathetic person."

Now, a big smile and a wider legspread from Basiliska.

My wife, Rudd, now appeared with our friend, whom I'll call Barbara Stanwyck. I introduce them to my new friends, but they take two chairs at the outer rim of our group and begin chattering away in fast English, oblivious to the social and linguistic swamp I am drowning in.

Suddenly, in the middle of the throng in the crowded room, I now spot an Italian woman who is a good friend. If I can catch her eye, she will help me out of this. "Maria," I yell out. "Maria Cacciatore!"

Maria sees me, waves, but I see in the sweep of her eye that she has taken in Il Duce sitting beside me, and the weather report does not look good for this evening.

I press on gamely. "Maria, this is my friend. He's Italian, from Rome."

"He's a son of a bitch," says Maria in English, and then to Benito in Italian, "*Ah, buonasera, signior.*" Benito frowns also. He does not seem pleased to see her either.

Maria comes over behind my chair, lowers her head and whispers to me confidentially. "That man is no good. He was having some difficulty at the purser's desk and when I tried to help him, he told me to get lost, that he didn't need anyone meddling into his life. So, he can go to hell, Roger. I'll talk to you later." With that, she turned away and launched into conversation with Rudd and Barbara.

I turned back to my charges. Basiliska was now making gurgling sounds of pleasure and Benito was now stating that surely she must have Italian blood in her somewhere.

"What? What?" demanded the goddess.

"He says surely you have Italian blood in you somewhere."

Basiliska's eyes whirled, "Well, maybe my great-grandfather . . ."

Benito, now quite plastered, wanted another drink.

"No, signior, you've had enough. The party's ending now."

Il Duce rose up in all his power now and shouted out to a waiter in Italian, "I demand another gin and tonic."

To my amazement, the waiter spoke Italian, and quite affably took the order.

I looked helplessly at Rudd and Barbara Stanwyck. "I'll meet you back in the stateroom," I said significantly to Rudd. "*Buonasera, signior.* Goodnight all." And I stumbled away, vowing never, never to go to another cocktail party on this voyage.

E-Mail from Verna Rudd Kenvin, Cabin No. 4127
To: Norma and Lou
Date: Saturday, March 24

. . . Your trip to Europe is getting close, but the end of our travels is also approaching. It has been a wonderful adventure, getting us to so many places we have wanted to see. Yesterday it was Mumbai (Bombay). I was pleasantly surprised to see what a lovely city it is. It was quite clean, has lots of trees, which provide shade, and, yesterday a cooling breeze to make the heat less oppressive.

I went on one tour, Roger another. Because my leg/knee and vertigo problems make it difficult for me to walk on uneven ground, we decided that I should take the city tour while he did the caves. I also will not do Petra in Jordan . . . .

. . . We still hope we will be able to go through the Suez Canal. We get a *New York Times Cruise Edition* on board ship that is quite good, but it does not necessarily provide all the news. . . .

Love,

Rudd and Roger

Gold Souk, Dubai, United Arab Emirates

MIRACLE IN ARABIA

"As for him who voluntarily performs a good work, truly God is grateful and knowing."

The Koran

One of the joys of traveling is arriving in a port like Dubai. Not too long ago this was just a desert oasis on the Persian Gulf with some tents and bedouins, part of what was called Arabia, but when oil was discovered a brand new city with some of the most modern, dazzling skyscrapers grew up and today Dubai is surely one of the wonders of the modern world.

It is only since 1971 that Dubai has come into its own. It is helped by having a benevolent sultan who fosters progress and social welfare so that the country is immaculately clean and prosperous looking. The Marine terminal was inaugurated by the arrival of the *Queen Elizabeth 2*, and it is surely the world's handsomest ship terminal at the moment.

For many years, Dubai, like other countries in the area, was under Great Britain's protection, part of the deal in guaranteeing England its passage to India. But after India was lost in 1947, the British quit this area in 1968, so that in 1971 seven states—Dubai, Ajman, Abu Dhabi, Fujaira, Ras-al-Khaimah, Sharjah, and Umm al-Qaiwain formed the current federation of United Arab Emirates. Both oil and international banking are their chief economic cards.

The total population is 2,369,153 in about 32,000 square miles. About 800,000 people live in Dubai.

The city lies on Dubai Creek, a natural inlet from the Persian Gulf, which divides the city into two parts, Deira and Bur Dubai. Once there was a lot of pearl fishing in this area, but today there are teak dhows, ferries, abras (water taxis), and boats of all kinds making the harbor a busy, festive place.

Among the stunning new skyscrapers are the World Trade Centre, 39-storeys tall, and the shimmering blue Telecommunications Building topped with a gleaming ball.

The Jumeirah Beach Hotel, a 600-room hotel designed as an enormous breaking wave with its conference and convention center in the shape of a giant dhow, is also a knockout piece of architecture, which prompted a number of QE2 passengers to make straight for it for breakfast, lunch, or drinks. Other deluxe hotels include the Hyatt Regency, the Ritz Carlton, the Sheraton, the Jebel Ali Hotel and the Dubai Marine

We took a ride in the harbor, marveling at the skyline, and then visited the old city, including the amazing Dubai Museum, with exhibits featuring realistic mannequins in dioramas recreating the old Arabian past, and we went to the house of Sheik Saeed, grandfather of the present Sheik. This was the official home of the ruling Al-Maktoum family. It was formally made into a museum in 1958. It is incorporated into the impressive Fort Al-Fahidi, beautifully positioned on a point of land, the fort dating from the early nineteenth-century. I think the current Sheik was educated at the University of California in Irvine, at least in part, which may help explain why he is so good as a leader.

Another interesting sight in the Bastakiya section were the homes with wind towers built into them. These caught the wind and brought it down into the courtyards. This method was an early Arabian form of air conditioning. Many of the homes looked very comfortable. I thought of parallels with homes in Santa Fe, New Mexico, also well suited to its particular geography and meteorology.

A memorable highlight in the old city was our visit to both the Spice Souk and the Gold Souk. The Spice Souk smelled especially good as I examined frankincense and myrrh in the pleasant mix of cinnamon, cardamon, cloves, nuts, and dried fruits of all kinds.

The brilliant Gold Souk had hundreds of shops with gold baubles of all sorts in them available at good prices. One could buy either the red-gold 24 karats, favored by Asians, or the yellow-gold 18 karats, preferred by Americans and Europeans.

The souks predictably were crowded with visitors, and I took many photographs there. Muslim women do not like to be photographed head on, and it is always good form to ask permission before photographing anybody. I found the inhabitants of the souks to be affable and often helpful. One even suggested that I photograph his neighbor merchant, who agreed, but shouted out to me, "Only if you put my photograph in a prominent place. I don't wish to be buried in the back pages."

In the middle of the city, we also saw the Jumeirah Mosque, its minarets punctuating the blue sky, but now looking a little out of place with the modern architecture surrounding it.

96% of Dubai residents are Muslim, but their religious practices are modern and not severe. Muslims in the Middle East usually explain to Westerners that their practices stem from local customs, not from the Muslim religion, as some Westerners erroneously think.

At the port, as part of the festivities inaugurating the Marine Terminal, Arabs set up exhibits illustrating typical activities of Dubai, such as boat building, basket weaving, games, camel riding, and falconry. Camel races take place on Thursdays and Fridays in the winter months, and Dubai even has a special falcon hospital.

Incidentally, Westerners might be interested to know that owning a camel can be very expensive. One camel can sometimes cost as much as one hundred thousand dollars. That puts it on a par with an expensive Mercedes Benz. A camel or a car?

Back on board the ship, dancers from Dubai performed some of the local dances in the Grand Lounge.

We also visited a large shopping mall in the center of town and were able to buy some needed medicines in an up-to-date, clean pharmacy.

I should mention also that horse breeding and horse racing are two other Dubai specialties. Dubai has two racecourses.

Our home in California is near the Santa Anita Racetrack, so that, after our return home, we began to notice how often the name "Dubai" came up. Now we understand more fully what's behind it.

ON SHIPBOARD

Overheard conversation on the Boat deck, one man to the other:

"Sorry. I meant to tell you who he was. He was a friend who, after he died, became an anecdote in our family."

FRANKINCENSE AND MYRRH

Oman is a neighbor of the United Arab Emirates and also has borders with Saudi Arabia and Yemen. For years it was known as Muscat and Oman until it became the Sultanate of Oman in 1970. Its population is about 2.5 million people.

The capital city is Muscat, but it is actually three cities in one—Muscat, the old port area; Mutrah, the trading area and harbor; and Ruwi, the commercial and administrative area. It is every bit as clean and attractive as Dubai, but it seems longer established, an appealing blend of the old and new, which are quite compatible here.

There are hills on three sides of Muscat, rocky, lacking vegetation, and there are two forts on the east and west, Fort Jalali and Fort Mirani. Both forts were built by Portuguese conquerors on the old Arab foundations, and both forts are used today by the army and the police.

We also visited the Sultan's palace nearby and saw the attractive homes of wealthy Omanis and some of the foreign embassies. The architecture of these homes is a nice blend of Arab, Portuguese, and Indian styles. They look very spacious and comfortable.

Noteworthy was a splendid blue-domed mosque here. The Omanis' brand of Islam is called Ibadhi and they elect their own Imams.

In Mutrah, we saw the fort built by the Portuguese in the 1580s. It sits in a commanding position on a cliff overlooking the Gulf of Oman.

We spent some time in the Mutrah souk where we bought a lapis lazuli pendant for our daughter, Heather's birthday, and, finally, I bought some real frankincense and myrrh to use in our Christmas decorations.

At Qurm, a former fishing village, we visited the Oman Museum, containing objects from the country's past.

Again, Oman was a pleasant experience. It has an extremely low crime rate, people we encountered were uniformly friendly, and the city streets were remarkably clean. I also admired the beautiful landscaping along the roads. There were many petunias and much imaginative topiary work in the hedges and plants. The roads and highways were all immaculate, considering that Muscat, like Dubai, is an oasis in a vast desert.

ON SHIPBOARD

From a window on the upper deck, I look out into the bright sunlight and see a sign that reads

PORT SULTAN
QABOOS

Behind this sign lies a brilliant Piet Mondrian arrangement—hundreds of containers fated to be loaded, brick red, green, grey, silver, mustard yellow, light blue, ultramarine—bound for mysterious ports all over the world. Their names and order of stacking make a natural poem right in front of my eyes:

Maersk		Global	
Sealand	Uniglory		UASC
Nedland	Matson	Pro	
Evergreen	NOL	Genstar	
Balaji	CMA	Triton	Seaco
Tiphok		Hapag Lloyd	

Huge, yellow, dinosaur lifts, three and four storeys high, glide by effortlessly on tracks.

A large, white ship with orange and blue trim and *Europa* painted on its side lies in wait, quiet as a crocodile.

Two squat freighters hog the pier, *Spar Two* and *Orient Patriot,* a blue ship already loaded with Maersk containers.

Moving in counterpoint, red, white, and green tugboats, the pushing, pulling, shoving experts.

Another freighter tolerantly joins the queue, *Al Qabil*, an invitation to Arabian nights.

E-Mail from Verna Rudd Kenvin, Cabin no. 4127
To: Brooke and David, Heather and Tom, Norma and
Lou, Joan and Rob
Date: Wednesday, March 28

. . . Thanks for all the Kyle and Dylan stories.
Please keep sending them. I did hear from Marcia
Garbus Burnam on the *Rotterdam*. She was off on a
three-day trip to New Delhi while we were in port at
Mumbai. She is having the experience of a lifetime.
She thanked us again for putting the idea into her
head when we saw her at David's publication party.
. . . At Mumbai, we had to take a launch into port in
a not-too-calm sea and a most difficult landing site. P
went to his Elephanta Caves tour, so he was not able
to help me. One of the men we have met became my
guardian angel.
     The buses were air-conditioned, thank goodness,
although old and dilapidated. Our guide was excellent,
however. What amazed me about Mumbai was how
clean it was and how many shade trees there are.
     Two most interesting sights were the Dhobi
Ghats and the Jain Temple. The ghats now have city
water, although they are still in the open air where
the drying is now done on the roofs of shacks. The
temple was very lovely, but not unlike many others.
     The big surprise was Dubai in the United Arab
Emirates. It was so very modern and immaculate. The
architecture is stunning. . . .
. . . We saw the Sultan of Dubai at the new marine
terminal after he had dedicated it. They waited for the

QE2's arrival. There was a royal red carpet, dancing children in gold-trimmed costumes, camels, and falcons.

The highlight of the Dubai tour was the Dubai Museum, all underground, showing how the people used to live only ten years ago, in huts, tents, no electricity, no city water, etc. There is also a nice river winding through the center of the city.

Muscat, Oman, was also an amazingly clean and new city, but the architecture was not as stunning, nor was it as clean and impressive as Dubai. It shows what money, mostly from oil, can do. . . .

Lots of love to all,

Rudd

E-Mail from Verna Rudd Kenvin, Cabin no. 4127
To: Heather, Brooke
Date: Friday, March 30

. . . Now for Colombo, Sri Lanka. We did dock, but it was a dreadfully hot and humid day. Our guide was terrible. He would not speak up even though he knew all the speakers were not working. He should have stood in the middle of the bus, as we asked him to, and used his natural voice, but he insisted on using the faulty equipment. Where P and I sat, we could hear, but the man was still not very informative.

When we arrived at their big museum, I remained in the bus, because the guide had said we would only have thirty minutes there, and I could see that it was a long walk to the entrance, about ten minutes' worth each way, so the time seemed far too short.

I did not go into the temple, either, at the next stop, because you have to take your shoes off and then put them on again afterward.

What I did notice, however, was a lot of soldiers with automatic machine guns at the ready, streets barricaded, and a boat with a long gun up front patrolling the QE2 from the waterside.

Later, I saw a white motor boat headed right where I was sitting. I was a bit alarmed. Needless to say, it turned away.

We did stop for tea at one of the old hotels, called the Galle Face Hotel. Ceiling fans, no air-conditioning, old retainers wearing the kind of colonial outfits our former cook, Rahat, in India, would have loved. I hope P took a picture of the doorman.

There was another tour into Kandy and the countryside, but it was eight hours long . . . . A friend of ours went and said the environment was very lush. They went to an elephant orphanage, too, which sounded intriguing. . . . .

. . . Lots of love to you and your families. You all have been great, helping us do all this.

Love,

Mom

TOGETHERNESS ON THE DESERT

*"When this one grows, the other shrinks, and when
The night is long, the day is not complete."*

Al-Ma'arri

We docked on the morning of April 1 at Aqaba in the Hashemite Kingdom of Jordan and toured the city, which did not take too long, since its population is only about 40,000 people, even though it is the second largest city in the country. The largest and capital city is Amman, population 1.4 million. King Abdullah II, eldest son of King Hussain, is the ruler.

We had hoped to go on one of the excursions to Petra, along with others from the QE2, but there was some question as to whether horses would be available for the difficult journey through the Bab es-Siq into Petra, so we canceled and confined our sightseeing to Aqaba alone.

Actually, the site of Aqaba was intriguing. Lying at the head of the Gulf of Aqaba off the Red Sea, it shares its geography with Eilat in Israel and the Sinai desert behind it, but Aqaba is five times larger than Eilat. I thought the two twin cities in two different countries should provide a good example of the possibility of harmonious cooperation in the Middle East.

In Aqaba, we went to the Aqaba Marine Science Station and saw parrot fish, clownfish, sharks, huge turtles and coral from the Red Sea. A major attraction in town was the remains of a sixteenth-century fortress, built on the ruins of a Crusaders' castle, featuring round towers, dungeons, and stables from the time when it was used as a caravanserai for travelers. The Hashemite coat of arms is clearly delineated above the main entrance.

When I tired of looking at relics of Jordan's past, I wandered out and into the city to see something of its present and lifestyle. Everything was sand, dry, hot, and sun, with clumps of palm trees piercing the sky.

The Moonstone Hotel attracted my attention because of its name and pink stone, and so I gravitated toward it, photographing some people and places along the way. Because of the hot, blowing wind, the drifting sand and the dessicated debris and little stones that littered my path, I walked gingerly, as though on eggshells around an abandoned, dried up swimming pool. I reached down once and picked up two small pieces of pink limestone to bring home to our grandsons. My general impression of Aqaba is that it was unkempt, compared to the busy, clean cities of Muscat and Dubai.

The mountains behind Jordan, however, are very interesting. Craggy, rocky, they change color with the sun and make a sharp contrast with the white sand found everywhere.

There was also some building going on in Aqaba. In recent years, it has gained fame as a beach resort, especially known for its diving and snorkeling. The big hotels outside town are the centers for this and are often called "The Jordanian Riviera."

As for the citizens of Jordan, they are 75% Palestinians who were displaced when Israel was created by the United Nations. The population is very young and the current unemployment rate is 23-24%.

Jordan's history includes King Solomon who mined copper there in 1000 B.C., the Romans who overpowered it in 106 A.D., the Christian Crusaders who took over Aqaba in 1116 A.D., Egypt and Syria who helped themselves to the territory in the 12th century, and, finally, Israel, which in 1994 signed a peace treaty with its neighbor. But its biggest problem always has been its geography. Jordan is 88% arid, so it is doomed forever to be a land of shifting sands.

ON SHIPBOARD

For one's pleasure, there are many activities aboard the QE2 each day. Some are constant; others are special. Here is one day's schedule:

8:00 a.m. You can run around the deck with Ian (please wear training shoes)—sneakers to Americans.

9:00 a.m. Iona will put you through exercises in the Fitness Centre (don't forget those training shoes).

9:30. You can be religious and talk with a rabbi, priest, or minister in the Chart Room, play table tennis, do a daily crossword puzzle, or try a daily brain teaser quiz in the library.

10:00 a.m. There's Team Trivia in the Grand Lounge; script reading for would-be actors in the Yacht Club; a lecture on Islam in the Theatre; a Spanish lesson with Thomas Quinones in the Golden Lion Pub; a Tap, Soft Shoe, and Broadway Showbiz class in the Queen's Room; a Computer Lecture with Harry and Evelyn Barkan in the Computer Centre; a Bridge Lecture in the Crystal Bar (Port Side); more exercises with David; and games, also in the Crystal Bar (Starboard Side).

11:00 A special lecture by Lord Wedgwood on the famous Wedgwood family and pottery in the Theatre; a rehearsal of the Passenger Talent Show in the Grand

Lounge; a class on Japanese Origami in the Golden Lion Pub; Golf putting up on the Sports Deck; Morning Make-up with cosmeticians in the Yacht Club; and another lecture by the Barkans in the Computer Centre.

At 12:15 p.m. the heavily attended dance class led by Warren and Daniella Smith begins in the Queens Room; another acting class starts in the Grand Lounge; Keith Trewhitt plays cocktail music on the piano in the Crystal Bar while harpist Jacqueline Dolan plucks away in the Chart Room and pianist Colin Lewis plays and sings in the Golden Lion Pub, all the while a Caribbean Band, Onlyne, is making pretty music out on the Upper Deck.

Then after lunch, at 2:00 p.m., the bridge players show up in force for a session with Beverly and Hal in the Crystal Bar; Rolonde Faucon, a charming French lady, offers watercolor painting lessons in the Queens Room; a preview of the Fine Art Auction is revealed in the Golden Lion Pub; and *The Godfather* movie is shown on the big screen in the Theatre.

2:30 brings a talk on the San Carlo Opera House in Naples by Peter Francis in the Grand Lounge; an historical walking tour of the ship by a staff person; the Art Auction in the Golden Lion Pub; Golf up on the Sports Deck; and more computer stuff, fitness exercises, games of all sorts, to which beginning Whist has now been added.

At 3:30 p.m., one has the choice of attending the Passenger Talent Show in the Grand Lounge, or watching a concert of the Berlin Philharmonic conducted by André Previn on the large screen in the Yacht Club.

4:30 means Bingo in the Grand Lounge with money prizes; or, if you prefer, Hi-Lo Aerobics in the Fitness Centre; or a chance to knit, sew, and chat with Elaine in the Crystal Bar.

At 5:30, Catholic Holy Mass is celebrated with the charming Irishman, Father Eugene Nee in the Theatre while Iona (of the training shoes, please!) is showing you how to stretch and relax in the Fitness Centre. Don't forget that Afternoon Tea is served in the very grand manner by white-gloved waiters in the Queens Room from 4 to 5:00 p.m.

After dinner, the QE2 Big Band plays in the Queens Room; *The Godfather* is repeated on the screen in the Theatre; there is dancing in the Yacht Club; and a special World Cruise Charity Showtime takes place in the Grand Lounge featuring performers drawn from the crew of the QE2. Charity donations buckets will be at the doors.

Each year QE2 crew and passengers contribute money to twenty different charities: A few of them are the Rumanian Children's Appeal, the Pattaya Orphange in Thailand, Sunshine Coaches for the Blind, Fiji Crippled Children's Society, Caritas Charity in Manila, and the Countess Mountbatten Hospice for Cancer.

And this is just one day's possibilities!

PORT TOWN ON THE RED SEA

We stopped first in Egypt at Safaga, which is a port on the Red Sea fairly close to Luxor, where some passengers went for an overnight to view the temples of Luxor and Karnak, which together made up the ancient capital of Thebes around 1500 B.C. The rest of us were free to visit the relatively small town of Safaga, although Colin Parker and others of the QE2 staff assured us "there's nothing really to see there."

They were right. We docked in a restricted port area with soldiers, guns, and tight security, and were told not to photograph any ships. A shuttle bus was provided to transport us into the town's Holiday Inn.

I saw miles of white desert all around, none of it clean. Trash and garbage lay everywhere, whether blown by the desert winds or tossed there by careless people, I don't know. I saw some building going on also, although several of the projects looked as though they had been abandoned in the middle of construction. There also were a great many private homes looking very inadequate and a few people peering out of doorways.

Safaga itself was like a little one-street desert town, a few shops, some brightly painted, and a desert Holiday Inn, providing a welcome respite from the sun and sand.

I walked around, taking a few photographs, looking into shops. Two shopkeepers were very cordial, chatting with us, posing for photographs, writing out things in Arabic for us. We bought little pyramids, obolisks, and a basalt cat god from them. They provided us with a good first impression of the Egyptian people.

At the port we were given a welcome by townspeople in a kind of carnival atmosphere. People danced in clown outfits, a man walked on stilts, schoolchildren pranced in local costumes, and we could see boats and other larger ships passing through the harbor en route to the Suez Canal.

APPOINTMENT IN GIZA

"The Cairo sky was crisscrossed with planes day and night. The incredible thing was that daily life in houses, offices, shops, and markets carried on as usual, even though planes were screaming incessantly overhead and explosions kept going off."

Naguib Mahfouz

April 3, 2001, we docked at Port Suez and were supposed to be whisked away in a caravan of buses to Cairo, but we had a long wait and were greatly delayed. It was explained to us that we had to go in a caravan of twenty buses with two armed guards in each bus, a lead security van with flashing lights, and another armed security bus at the rear.

The Abercrombie & Kent people had to phone ahead to get special permission to keep the pyramids at Giza open after 4:00 p.m. especially for the QE2 people. Somebody from the ship was able to cut through the red tape to get this done.

It must have taken us an hour and a half to two hours to make the trip into Cairo. We once again crossed what is really the north Sahara desert. We passed many military camps with heavily armed guards. I saw tanks, mounted guns, and all the trappings of a military regime. We were also stopped several times, boarded by armed soldiers, and asked to show our passports, this being the only country in which we had to use them.

Fortunately, our Egyptian guide was excellent, an intelligent young mother of two named Eman. She came from Alexandria and was pleased when I asked her about the excavations there and the famous library ruins which are under water. Eman graduated from Alexandria College where she studied archaology and the Egyptian, English, French, and Italian languages. Her two sons were three and four years old.

It was late when we arrived in busy, hectic Cairo, and so we were taken right away to lunch at the Nile Hilton on Tahrir Square. This is next to the legendary Egyptian Museum, to which we walked.

Eman acted as our guide here also. Her focus was particularly on King Tutankhamun, but Rudd and I had waited five and a half hours in line in Washington, D.C. years ago to see those treasures, and now we were seeing them again. The Museum itself is an old Victorian palace, quite dark, with a lot of reverberation, not really the best venue for these relics.

Near the end of the day we ventured into the mainstream of Cairo traffic, completely chaotic, considering that the city has 13 million people, making it the largest city in Africa and the Middle East, and our bus took us out to the suburb of Giza, over the rooftops of which the pyramid tops loomed.

The whole desert, on a high plain, has the appearance of a park and is treated as such. Our buses were the only ones allowed in. Men on camels rode around posing for photographs. Police on camels chased them when they pestered people too much. There were also a few vendors at the site selling souvenirs of all kinds and bartering with visitors.

The three principal pyramids in Giza are the Great Pyramid of Cheops, about which it is said that one-hundred thousand men worked twenty years to build it. This pyramid is 450 feet high and one can enter into an empty funerary passage if one is willing to stoop. I wasn't.

The Pyramid of Khephren is a little smaller, but it stands on higher ground, and so it appears taller than it really is. It has a worn spot near the top which reveals the polished stone underneath. The pharaoh whose tomb this was is the reason the Sphinx was built—as a guard to this tomb. It is believed that the Sphinx' face was a likeness of Khephren himself.

The Pyramid of Mycerinus, 204 feet high, is the smallest of the three tombs. All three of these pyramids were constructed around 2600 B.C.

The sun was setting when we went around to study the Sphinx. Once it had been completely covered by sand from the desert, but Thutmose IV, who lived from 1425-1508 B.C. had the sand cleared to assure that he would become pharaoh. The damage done to the Sphinx' nose is said to have been done by the conquering Turks who used it for target practice because the Muslims did not believe in graven images.

I thought the Sphinx looked very impressive, about as threatening as a large Bengal tiger or lion you might see in a zoo—ominous, strong, yet quiet and enigmatic. I saw it as a symbol of the great Egyptian civilization and culture from which it sprang.

I thought of the layers of the past behind any Egyptian's experience—the Hyksos invaders, the Libyan invaders, the Nubians and Assyrians, the Persians, Alexander the Great and the Greek invaders, the Roman invaders, the Christians, the Arabs, the Turks with their Ottoman Empire, Napoleon and France, the British, then the Nazi General Rommel, who was defeated at El Alamein, and finally Israel. Is there any nation that hasn't had a piece of Egypt at one time or the other? I am not forgetting, either, the treasures of Egypt that I first saw in the permanent collections of museums in New York and London.

I liked seeing the muddy Nile in the middle of Cairo bisecting it into two halves, and flowing for over 600 miles through the African desert.

Now that darkness had fallen, we had to retrace our steps. About Cairo traffic, Eman had said, "The only driving rule Cairenes obey is 'fill in the empty spaces.'"

Other incidental information about Egypt gleaned from Eman is that ancient Egypt was divided into two kingdoms, the upper kingdom and the lower kingdom. The lower kingdom was the Nile delta, which flooded every year and included the cities of Alexandria and Cairo; the upper kingdom included the southern part of Egypt.

Eman also estimated Egypt's total population at 67 million and said Cairo had 15 million people, but on working days probably 17 million. She said the rainfall was only one inch of rain per year in Alexandria and she told us that water from the Nile River was filtered through 15 treatment plants, that there were 33 bridges across the Nile in Cairo, and that the name of the suburb by which we entered Cairo was called Heliopolis, the city of the sun.

Our bus driver drove home at breakneck speed, honking his horn frequently as all the other drivers did. A near tragedy was averted when he sideswiped a car driven by a young woman. We had to stop while our armed guards, driver, and an ashen-faced Eman got out to inspect the damage. They reported that the young woman driving the car had not been hurt, but that her car had been heavily damaged.

We rode back quite silently to Port Suez and climbed aboard the tender that took us back to the QE2. Tomorrow we would head up the Suez Canal to the Mediterranean and more familiar territory.

ON SHIPBOARD

"At every word a reputation dies."

Alexander Pope

For this world cruise, a special lounge was set up for the 425 people going all the way around. What is normally the Board Room high up on the Boat Deck in the posh part of the ship where the penthouse suites and the captain's quarters are was taken over and made into a comfortable lounge, complete with hostesses, tea, coffee, soft drinks, hors d'oeuvres, sandwiches, newspapers, sofas, easy chairs, and windows from which to peer at other mortals strolling on the open deck.

When one needed an exclusive retreat from the sometimes busy world of shipboard life, one could slip in there, have a quiet tea or chat with some global pioneer or other. You might discover something in common—a college or university, a surname, a town in Indiana, a successful friend, a book you both like.

Often, my reason for entering this domain was that I simply was hot and tired from the sun and humidity on deck and liked the air-conditioning and the free coca colas the hostess would bring. So I, being naturally quiet and reserved, was in a unique position to overhear what seemed to me bizarre conversations.

My favorites were two aging southern belles who held court and verbally assassinated other passengers. One lady had a sweet, round Olivia-de-Havilland-as-

Melanie-Wilkes face, but none of Melanie's integrity. The first time I saw this woman, whom I'll call South Carolina Susan, she had black hair. Later, on the voyage, it turned brunette, then grew blonder, until one day she had platinum hair framing her Melanie smile.

The other woman with her was older, far more conservative in appearance, a kind of Katherine Graham-type woman, a little awkward, but dressed always in good quality fabrics, and wearing very modest, but tasteful jewelry. I'll call her Estelle.

Susan's flamboyant style was to sit sidesaddle in her easy chair, toss her hair back, throw one arm around the back of the chair and say in a fairly clear voice, as though she were in a Noel Coward play, "Estelle, I just cannot believe you didn't notice that. Didn't you see how her face as well as her hair was pulled back just as far as it would go? I mean, yes, her complexion's as smooth as silk, but I know that's the result of all those face lifts. Yes, she's had a skin peel too. You can always tell. Gives her that stewed apple look. Skin is simply not that boiled pink color."

Estelle: "I thought she was very nice, though. And I like her husband."

Susan: (snorting) "Husband? My dear, that was only the fair game she was stalking at lunch in the Lido. He's just one of her caddies in another game of QE2 golf."

Estelle: "I thought he was being very considerate, pulling out that chair for her, and all. I admire a man with manners."

Susan: (hissing) "That's what a caddie's supposed to do. She uses him to get to other men. Men with money."

Estelle: "I think she's cute. She has that petite, hourglass figure. You've got to admit that."

Susan: "She's a ferret. She doesn't eat anything. She nibbles air. Just teases that pineapple on her plate and sips that vile lemonade. Ugh! She's as thin as Calista Flockhart, only she's seventy-two years old. She's as ruthless as . . . "

Estelle: "I'd like some more tea, dear. Could you ask Uta, please?"

And then Uta, a gracious hostess would come and pour the ladies another cup of tea so that they could continue with their malice-toward-everybody gossip.

Rudd had a theory that Susan was a paid traveling companion to the older, wealthier Estelle. She may have been right.

FOLLOW THE LEADER THROUGH SUEZ

We were underway well before 6:00 a.m. and did not complete the 117 mile voyage until 3:30 p.m. The *Queen Elizabeth 2* was the lead ship in the convoy of twenty ships permitted to sail through, each spaced one mile apart. The crossing usually takes fifteen hours, which is three hours longer than it takes to go through the Panama Canal.

Both Suez and Panama are famous for the time and distance they save ships in their respective areas, but the similarity ends there. Panama is a man-made feat of engineering, in which ships go through a series of locks, with a lake in the middle, and cross from one ocean to another.

Suez, on the other hand, appears to be a long ribbon through the desert, or a river. Man has had to work on it over the centuries, but it has been mainly to dredge it and clear it of the shifting sands the winds blow over it.

The modern Suez Canal is largely the work of Ferdinand de Lesseps, a French engineer, who began his work in 1859. It was opened in 1869 by the Empress Eugenie, and most recently was closed from 1967 to 1975 because of Israeli-Egyptian hostilities. It was nationalized by Egypt in 1956.

What I saw of the land on either side of the ship was at first very flat and the canal very straight. All along the way on either side I could see armed sentries in boxes at fairly regular intervals. Little villages began appearing, a very few boats, only isolated unwaving people occasionally. I could see blue and purple mountains through the morning sky in the distance. Then the landscape changed on both sides and became a blindingly white desertscape with undulating dunes, looking like something from *Lawrence of Arabia*.

Two war memorials, loomed up, piercing the sky, reminding one of the heavy bombing by Israel. One monument had a legend inscribed on it, reading *"Defense du Canal de Suez."* The other was in the shape of a sharply pointed missile aiming up.

Finally, we reached the end, having sailed from Port Suez up to Port Said and into the Mediterranean.

Since it makes the connection between Europe and India shorter and quicker, one could see why Suez has been so much fought over and debated.

I was surprised, as I was by everything in Egypt, to learn how jumpy the Egyptians were, and how militarily ready they were to retaliate, should Israel (with its great benefactor, the United States of America, behind it) ever attack them again. There quite clearly is a lot of understandable fear, distrust, religious, and cultural hatred in the Middle East, and not enough responsible leadership to help solve the problem. Egypt's great leader Anwar Sadat was assassinated in 1981.

What price, peace and cooperation in the Middle East?

ON SHIPBOARD

COMPLAINT DEPARTMENT
(Or don't let those chocolates on your pillow every
night deceive you)

After you have been on the QE2 for a while, you
may discover a few things that puzzle you and others
that annoy you.

One of the most puzzling aspects to me is the
curious English method of setting the table with an
armada of cutlery and then pulling off knives, forks,
spoons, whatever, according to what the passenger
chooses to eat at each meal. Actually, I have no
reason to complain now since I grew up in a British
household where, when I was young, my mother used
to set out table items the night before, and where my
Scottish relatives did this routinely.

But on the QE2, at dinner, for example, the
menu is designed for people who want to plough
through four or five courses. I eat sparingly, taking
only an appetizer, entrée, and dessert, with coffee
after. Night after night, the waiter would gather up
enough cutlery from my place to melt down into silver
bricks. And, since I ate fish a lot, that idiotic fish fork
the English have would always be flung down after the
regular knife had been removed.

Where does that unused cutlery go, I wondered?
Back into the bin from whence it came? And how
many people handle the cutlery you get at each meal?
I began to picture hundreds of British waiters making
a human chain, passing along knives, forks, and
spoons all the way to the galley.

Then there is the matter of that over-large oval spoon used for dessert, always lying perpendicularly to your dinner plate. Try using that clumsy utensil in those dainty compote dishes they give you for trifle and sherbets.

But this complaint pales beside the British method of using those utensils, which you must follow aboard ship if you want to avoid disapproving glances.

Grasp the fork in your left hand, tines down, and in your right hand wield the knife in as dextrous a manner as you can. Never drop either, but click them together over every morsel of food, and, imitating a talented gerbil or hamster, make quiet, scratching and cutting sounds, transferring tiny bits of food by way of your fork, tines down, to your mouth, which you close firmly as soon as food enters it.

During the meal, routinely exclaim "thank you" when you can (aim this at anybody who looks like a waiter), and at the end, smile successfully to others at the table, say, "Well, now, will you excuse me, please?" and then vanish quickly.

We have encountered more than once travelers who refuse to travel on any British ship because of what they call "the class system," but, when I tell them that has largely disappeared, they still book on one-class ships anyway, a favorite being the Holland-America Line.

Years ago in 1953, the first ship I ever crossed the Atlantic on was the Cunard Line's original *Queen Elizabeth*. This ship had three classes: first, cabin, and tourist, and the ship had physical barriers set up so that you could not pass from one area to the other without jumping over gates.

Once in 1955, we were traveling from Cobh, Ireland to New York on Cunard's *Britannic*, which had two classes, tourist and first, and the usual barriers. We were traveling tourist, but some friends of ours in first class invited us to the first class gala evening. To accomplish this, we had to vault the gates in full evening dress and then return the same way. It made us feel like the Downstairs part of *Upstairs, Downstairs* on Servants Night Off.

The good news is that the barriers have gone, but never underestimate Cunard. They know just how to get around such politically correct restrictions.

One way is via the dress code. I have already indicated that we had 44 formal evenings on this cruise. For them, I brought my white dinner jacket, full tuxedo, three evening shirts, five ties, three cummerbunds, one evening vest. My wife brought two long black skirts and eight different tops.

For other evenings, the dress code is Informal, which Cunard defines as "ties and jackets" for the men.

And yet another category is "Smart casual," which is anybody's guess, and then finally "casual," which is just fine for those who probably shouldn't have signed up for this ship in the first place.

The British do not like denim in any form, and so I always leave my bluejeans and cowboy boots behind when on a British ship and I usually forgo such American foods as hamburgers and hotdogs. which, so help me, the British eat, with knife and fork making those little cutting motions that form that distinctive "We're British" clicking sound in the dining room.

The dining room. That is where the British triumph, and where Queen Victoria, not Elizabeth reigns supreme. Where you dine on the QE2 conveys your social status instantly to the world aboard ship. At the top of the line is the Queens Grill where "every meal is an epicurean masterpiece," according to

Cunard. This is followed by the Princess Grill and the Britannia Grill, then the Caronia Restaurant, and finally the largest, the Mauretania, which has two sittings, early and late. According to Cunard, the Caronia "offers delightful menus and memorable cuisine," while the Mauretania features "exciting menus."

In actuality, the kitchen is the same for the Caronia and the Mauretania, as are all the menus in these two restaurants. Periodically, Cunard switches these two dining rooms around, so that if you have taken this ship as often as we have, you have probably dined in both these rooms.

A well-traveled friend of ours from New York has been on every level of accommodation there is and in every single dining room on the QE2. She maintains that there is not all that much difference from the Queens Grill on down, so she books on the Mauretania level now.

For this world cruise, we booked at the top M-1 class and I found the food excellent throughout.

I should mention, also, that there is a cafeteria called The Lido in the stern of the ship, where those who cannot stand dress codes at all can take all their meals in relative ease, except of course for shorts, T-shirts, and blue jeans at dinner. Incidentally, sometime during any QE2 voyage, an old line Brit will bend your ear with the complaint that "it's not the same, is it? It's all become so Americanized." When you say, "In what way?" the Brit will usually gesture toward the Lido and say *sotto voce*, "Oh, well, you know, carrying those trays and all. Self service. Not quite proper, is it? Not what you'd expect."

Your restaurant category rides with you throughout the voyage. You are P-2, C-1, Q-2 (You get a butler with this one), or in our case, M-1 (Better than M-2, M-3, M-4, or M-5, I suppose). Your ticket and all tags carry your brand. "What, you're M-4 people? My mistake. I thought you were B-1s, like us."

One day, lolling in my cabin, or what passes for lolling in an M-1 cabin, I thought of all the ways in which Cunard unsubtly still perpetuates the class system. Here is what I discovered, made into a list, another gift from crass America, I guess:

1) The staterooms are notoriously small on the QE2, but we chose the ship because it is exactly that—a ship—not one of those generic American motels with verandahs and vending machines down the hall so burping, farting Americans can haul ice for their drinks, corpses, or whatever at all hours of the nights. Our stateroom was #4127, an outside cabin with a porthole in the choice midship "E" stairway area. Our beds were two built-in bottom bunk beds, uncomfortable mattresses, slanted so that I fell out of bed three times on the voyage.

We had two very narrow closets for our clothes, three months' worth, including all those fine duds for 44 hotshot formal evenings.

My closet had a safe for me to store valuables and papers in it, a nice convenience, but who was the smartass who installed it at ankle level in the back of the closet, which meant that everytime I used it I had to stoop, kneel, bend in, ruffle my hair on hanging trousers to open the safe which was keyed to my American Express credit card which had to be slid along in a groove I could not see and which did not always work?

Underneath the safe was a shoe rack that would hold only three pairs of shoes. I had four pairs of shoes, plus slippers.

In the stateroom itself, we had two chests of drawers, but the drawers were shallow, inadequate to hold all our belongings. One chest was positioned between the two beds. When you pulled the drawers straight out, you could not sit in that area on either bed, but had to slide down near the ends of the beds. Also, if two people sat on both beds opposite each other, you would lock legs, so you always had to sit sidesaddle.

2) In the bathroom, when one sat on the toilet in an extremely narrow area, the toilet paper holder gouged one in the left ribs. Similarly, the shower stall was so narrow, one could not readily turn around in it.

3) All overhead lighting was inadequate in the stateroom. There were no reading lights. In the bathroom, the only light was the overhead. There was no light on the mirror. It was impossible for me to shave by. Apparently, all this low light was by design. There was a notice saying they were conserving power or something by doing this.

4) The door to the bathroom could not be opened when the door to the outside corridor was open. They would lock in a noisy battle of clashing iron wills.

All these quaint aspects combined to give me the impression that I should have paid more money to Cunard for what I regard as fairly basic necessities. Remember, we chose and still choose Cunard over all the others, but it is important to understand that sometimes I felt as though I had been sentenced to this ship as punishment for something I did wrong.

As England's venerable Dr. Samuel Johnson might have put it, "Well, you're correct there, Roger. You had no business being an American in the first place."

E-Mail from Verna Rudd Kenvin, Cabin no. 4127
To: Brooke, Heather, Rob and Joan
Date: Tuesday, April 3

Hello to all you faithful E-mail senders. It is now 7:45 a.m., April 3. Do not ask the day because I am very sleepy. We are now cruising at a very slow speed through the Suez Canal. We apparently are the lead ship because there are ships behind us and none in front. We go in convoys of twenty ships at a time, single file. Ships can only go through in one direction at a time.

It is rather neat having this majestic ship lead the pack, but maybe they think it is safer that way. I mean it seriously.

Yesterday when we took our tour to Cairo and the pyramids, our bus had to wait until all buses were loaded, so that we could travel in a convoy with a lead car flashing lights and two security men in the front seats of every bus. We passed oodles of garrisons with armed soldiers peering out of towers. A bit eerie. Yet, coming back, we did not need to be in a convoy, although the security officers stayed with us all day.

But to get back to the canal. It is quite narrow most of the way. On the west side, one sees very flat fields, but a lot of green (This is the delta area of the Nile River, although not the Nile) and many armed soldiers in little sentry boxes. On the east side, it is flat with sand and more sand.

Markers are posted every 100 kilometers. I think the canal is somewhere between 107-120 miles long with no locks, unlike the Panama Canal. This Suez passage is just a smooth, steady ride.

I have already walked a quarter of a mile on deck this morning, surveying the scene. I thought I should send off this note as a commemorative edition. Also, in case something dreadful happens, you will know we got to see the pyramids and the Suez Canal, two of our main goals on this trip.

We almost did not get to see the pyramids because while we were at anchor at Port Suez, the water was very choppy with 30 miles-per-hour winds. That made it unsafe for the launches to go in. We had awakened at 5:30 a.m. to get ready to depart at 7:15 a.m., but we did not actually leave until 11:30 a.m. . . We had a super guide, college-educated in anthropology, history, languages, and art . . .

After lunch, we did the museum. The photographs make it look like the British Museum where we saw the Rosetta Stone several years ago. Photos lie. This Cairo museum was cramped and dusty. But what treasures! . . . . The place was jammed, mostly by QE2 people, I think, and there were many guides, all shouting to their groups. P and I were not able to hear everything that was said, but enough to appreciate what we were seeing. There were incredible alabaster items, gold legs on many objects, exquisite inlay on jewelry boxes. All that for the afterlife, but nothing for improving people's lives in the present. Religion surely gave a huge helping hand to the top dogs. . . .

From the museum, we drove through a dirty, dilapidated Cairo out toward the pyramids. Suddenly, we were looking at unfinished apartment houses by the dozen, and the next thing we knew there was sand and the pyramids. We drove up a special road, along with the other buses. We were very late, near sunset, because of our delay at the beginning.

Men were riding around on their camels. Some were security guards with guns; others were camel cowboys who just wanted to sell camel rides or pose for photographs, for a price, of course. Occasionally, the police would ride up and pull them away from reluctant tourists. Since everything was so different from what I expected, I was slow taking it all in.

We could not walk close to Cheop's pyramid to assess its size, but our guide told us that Shaquille O'Neal's height reaches about a foot below the edge of the first layer of stones.

We saw many more pyramids than I thought we would, some in various stages of crumbling, others still being unearthed. And, in the near distance, Cairo's tall buildings.

We drove down to the site of the Sphinx. Another disappointment since photographs make it seem gargantuan. It is big and very impressive, but different from most photos of it. As we watched the Sphinx with several pyramids in the background, the sun began to set behind the clouds. Very dramatic. This is why these objects were placed on the West bank of the Nile. The East is for the living, the West is for the dead.

A few sentries on camels were silhouetted in the distance on the very top of a large sand dune. That was a fantastic sight.

Our trip back to the ship through the night was illuminated periodically by neon-decorated mosques and apartment clusters. The driving was not to be believed or desired. A woman driving a car cut in front of our bus, and our driver swerved over the curb and back onto the highway, but he hit her car sideways. The woman was not hurt, but her car and the bus both suffered damage. It was 9:30 p.m. and it left me a bit shaken since I saw it coming. . . .

Our visits to Aqaba and Safaga were interesting in their own ways. Still lots of guns, soldiers, police all around, plus some gun boats ready to go. Aqaba faces Eilat, Israel, at the tip of the Gaza strip. We sent some postcards from Aqaba where some of the postage stamps were incredibly lovely.

Today should be fairly restful and so should tomorrow while we are on our way to Naples, Herculaneum, and Capri again. We are winding down now, literally counting the days until we dock in New York. At the moment, though, we anticipate bursting into the Mediterranean where, I know, we will breathe a sigh of relief after all this military background. But if we don't make it safely through Suez, just remember that we were doing what we have always wanted to do.

Lots of love from us both,

Mom/Rudd

CHE BELLEZZA, ITALIA

Maria Cacciatore was ecstatic as we docked at the Stazione Maritima in Naples. "I can hardly wait to fight with the Neapolitans," she said, clenching her fists in a mock boxing stance. "I just love those faces!"

I understood exactly what she meant. Naples has always meant faces to me, too. There is plenty of toughness here, starkly dramatic Anna Magnani character, survivor-takes-all durability. I have always loved taking black-and-white photographs here, mostly of people, rarely of buildings and monuments. No wonder Italian filmmakers like DeSica, Fellini, and Rossellini came here to shoot their *verismo* films in the aftermath of World War II.

But, on the first day, I decided to revisit Herculaneum to check on the progress made in excavating it. I had last visited it seventeen years earlier. As everyone knows, in 79 A.D. Mount Vesuvius erupted, burying Pompeii under volcanic ash which had the effect of preserving people and objects in it and sending heavy mud down in a slide that buried the seaside resort of Herculaneum in a coating so thick that it made a kind of iron-clad casing around the ancient city.

Pompeii had been a large commercial center, but Herculaneum was a posh resort where wealthy Neapolitans built lavish seaside homes for themselves and their families. One of these was the father of Calpurnia, wife of Julius Caesar. Centuries later, Jean-Paul Getty used the plans for this Herculaneum home as the basis for the first Getty Museum in Malibu, California. The setting and the climate, as well as the house and grounds, duplicate quite precisely the original Herculaneum setting.

Since it was a summer resort for about four or five thousand inhabitants, it had a small agora, a large swimming pool and gymnasium, substantial summer villas, many with interesting mosaics on the walls.

The town was officially dedicated to and named after Hercules, half god, half man. In mosaics there, Hercules is always depicted as a dark-skinned man. No temples to any Roman deities have ever been found in Herculaneum. Of course, the town was originally Greek in origin.

Because of the thickness of the hardened mud, only about twenty percent of Herculaneum has been excavated. I was astonished at how little progress they have made over recent years. The theatre is a case in point. They were digging it out seventeen years ago, but it is still unearthed because the soil is leaking toxic gas, so it cannot be opened to the public yet.

Our guide here was Franco, 6'4", very well-informed on archaology, history, and art.

What is particularly striking about Herculaneum is that the old town is sixty feet down in the ground and the new town is built directly on top of it. You can stand way down in the ruins, look up at the bustling new city and see the culprit, Vesuvius, in the distance.

We also took a whirlwind bus tour through modern Naples passing familiar places from our previous visits in 1954 and 1984, the Castel Nuovo, San Carlo Opera House, the Palazzo Reale, the

Duomo and all the colorful piazzas and parks that make you want to become a filmmaker on the spot.

At night in the Grand Lounge on board ship, some Italian dancers did folk dances and tarantellas for the passengers.

On the next day, April 7, we sailed out to Capri, and once again toured that charismatic town and went up by bus to Anacapri to visit the home and gardens of Dr. Axel Munthe, a Swedish physician, who had settled there many years ago, collecting antiquities, writing about Capri and popularizing it as an international tourist attraction.

The drive up to Anacapri was fairly hair-raising, similar to the drive along the Amalfi coast, and, oddly, the day was cold and windy. Fortunately, we had brought our windbreakers with us which were a godsend on this very uncomfortable day.

Dr. Munthe's house and gardens were very carefully arranged, as you might expect, something like living in a museum with well-chosen statues, mosaics, and tasteful paintings on the wall, combined with a kind of Swedish selectivity—nothing in excess.

The views from Anacapri were superb. One remembered that Emperor Nero had had Christians thrown off the cliffs here, a reminder that terrible deeds can be done in beautiful settings.

Back in Capri we had lunch at a restaurant and then wandered through the town. Rudd was tired so I suggested she sit on the terrace of the Quisisana Hotel and have a drink. I would meet here there later.

I continued on to the unusually elegant garden of the Emperor Augustus overlooking the Faraglioni rocks at the end of Capri and then stopped at the Quisisana on the way back for a drink with Rudd.

We first visited Capri back in 1954, and several times later. It hasn't really changed much—a gorgeous island where wine usually is cheaper than water. Its famous Blue Grotto is still a major attraction, the water inside it an unbelievable silver-blue, typifying the theatrical, romantic quality of this legendary isle.

In 1984, when my mother and daughter Brooke traveled with us, we sent them off in a boat with a singing oarsman into the Blue Grotto. Once you visit Capri, you are certain to return sometime in your future.

ON SHIPBOARD

I spied Maria Cacciatore and her friend Laura trying to round up deck chairs on the Boat Deck for themselves. I said, "May I help you, Maria?" and she looked helplessly at a deck chair on which someone had left a towel and magazine.

"Just move it," I said. "They are not supposed to hold chairs that way."

"That is a no-no on this ship," replied Maria. "It could lead to bloodshed."

I told Maria and Laura that on the *Vistafjord* in the Pacific there had been some Germans aboard who followed the sun by leaving their belongings on at least three different chairs in strategically sunny locations on deck and that this had bothered the English greatly because Cunard specifically requested that people not reserve chairs in that manner.

"Let me tell you," said Maria. "Just yesterday we had an international incident. A little Spanish man who spoke no English plunked down his stuff on two adjoining deck chairs, and then he went away. Another man came along, moved the Spaniard's stuff off both chairs to the deck, sat down in one of the chairs for a few minutes, looked at his watch, and left. Shortly afterward, a couple of innocents appeared, a husband and wife, who saw two vacant chairs and settled comfortably into them.

"Finally, the Spaniard returned, saw his belongings scattered and two strangers sitting in his chairs. He began berating them in Spanish, which they didn't understand."

"The innocent husband rose up from his chair and the Spaniard raised his arm to hit him. The innocent grabbed the Spanish man's arm to prevent him from striking, whereupon Don Quixote, in high indignation, zipped open his fly, pulled out his penis and waved it at the husband, as though to ward off evil."

"They should have thrown Quixote into the brig," exclaimed Laura.

"That's what I said," replied Maria, "but at breakfast this morning there he was in the dining room, just as though nothing had happened."

Laura looked at me, rolling her eyes. "That's our select QE2 group for you," she laughed. Thus ended the saga of *El Caballero del Golpe Falo*.

Cours Mirabeau, Aix-en-Provence

AN ARTIST'S LIFE FOR ME

"Why doesn't the past decently bury itself, instead of sitting patiently waiting to be admired by the present?"

D. H. Lawrence

April 9, 2001: The ship docked at Marseille, France's second largest city, a great port city we had visited several times before, the setting for Marcel Pagnol's trilogy, *Fanny, Marius*, and *Cesar.*

In the morning I went to Arles, specifically to see the Roman ruins. We went first to Arènes, the Roman amphitheatre dating from the first century A.D. It is 456 feet long and 351 feet wide. It originally featured gladiators and wild beasts, but is used today primarily for bullfighting.

Next I saw the ruins of the antique Roman theatre, very much toppled over in a parklike setting with many trees, and very disappointing as a result. In the summer, plays and pageants are presented there.

Our guide concentrated on the Eglise St. Trophime, a church in the Romanesque style, named after the bishop who first brought Christianity to the area in the third century A.D., and its adjoining cloister with its sculpted capitals depicting scenes from the life of Jesus and other glimpses of mediaeval religious life, but I was much more interested in the village square with the Café de la Nuit, painted a strong yellow color, which was frequented by artist Vincent Van Gogh during the year he lived in Arles, and the statue of poet Frederic Mistral, who won the Nobel Prize for Literature and sparked renewed interest in Provencal literature and the language, which differs somewhat from French.

For lunch we went by bus up to Les Baux de Provence, one of France's "perched villages", as our guide Anne-Marie referred to them, nestled like birds' nests on the sides or tops of mountains. Les Baux is very white looking, being constructed from limestone found widely in this part of Provence. The town seems to spring right out of its natural setting. Les Baux is very picturesque indeed, dating back as far as the fifth century, a prime example of how natural rock became a mighty citadel.

We entered through the Porte Mage, a magnificent stone gate with the town hall to one side, now used as a museum, attesting to the tradition that the lords of this citadel came back from the Crusades as the heirs of Balthasar, the wise man who is supposed to have brought gold to the Christ child.

I also walked briefly out around the Alpilles Mountains and saw the old Chateau and the village church, Eglise St. Vincent, from the twelfth century, also constructed out of white limestone. In the distance in the mountains was the long outline of Montagne Sainte-Victoire, a major theme in the paintings of Paul Cezanne.

We had lunch at the Hotel Reine Jeanne, the meal consisting of fish paté, duck a l'orange, chocolate dessert, demi-tasses of coffee, reminding one how superb French cuisine really is, and I had a chance to rattle on un-selfconsciously in French, feeling right at home after being so lost in Asian and Arabic languages.

On the next day, April 10th, Rudd went to visit Cassis, a little fishing village favored by artists like Matisse and Dufy. Her leg was troubling her and she was afraid there might be too much walking in Aix-en-Provence, which was where I was headed for the day. She was right, but Aix was the perfect choice for me.

AIX-EN-PROVENCE

The minute we landed in Aix-en-Provence, I fell in love with it, as almost everybody does. It is exactly the way you would want the ideal French town to look. A wide main street, the Cours Mirabeau, lined with elegant plane trees against architecturally-striking buildings from the 17th and 18th centuries. Four fountains lining the way from the grand Rotonde fountain (1860, although there were earlier fountains on the site as far back as 1728) which has a stone figure of Justice as a woman facing the Cours Mirabeau in the general direction of the prison and the law courts; Agriculture facing across the landscape to the port city of Marseille; and Beaux Artes facing Avignon, dignified, ancient seat of culture and once home to popes.

Then, as you amble up the Cours, La Fontaine des Neuf Canons (1691) which I think was originally dedicated to St. Lazarus and from which some people still get drinking water; La Fontaine d'Eau Chaude (1734) featuring the curative water that made the town famous as a spa pouring out over a moss-covered lump of stone which M.F.K. Fisher called "Old

Mossback" and described as looking like "an elderly and benevolent dog, a little steamy and pungent;" and then, finally, the Fountain of King René, from 1820, showing the beloved king with a bunch of Muscat grapes in his hand, since he introduced them to the region.

Branching off from the Cours Mirabeau are numerous winding streets and alleys, like the Agard Passage, which takes one to the Palais de Justice. Some of these streets are faintly mysterious, full of pedestrians bent on secret missions, and quaint little shops, but which will plunge one out again into some gorgeous square full of sunshine and provencal beauty when you least expect it.

Near the Agard Passage on the Cours Mirabeau is the Café Les Deux Garcons (The Two Waiters), dating from 1792, a great favorite of painter Paul Cezanne, whose hometown Aix is, and of countless thousands ever since.

M.F.K. Fisher, in her book *Two Towns in Provence*, writes lovingly of this café and town in which she lived for several years with her two daughters. Her portraits of Madame Lanes, her imperious French landlady, with her stereotypical notions of Americans, and the bizarre Gypsy Woman who held her daughters in some kind of fearful spell and would make The Sign whenever she spotted them in Les Deux Garcons with their mother, are unforgettable.

Equally memorable are Fisher's portraits of the charismatic Dr. Vidal and the ex-law professor, Brondino, who operated an eccentric bookstore in Aix, specializing in posters and allowing Modern Art to take over his shop until his death on April Fools Day in 1961. He and his shop were lodestones for Fisher. She said he was a "scabrous and even destructive rebel."

Les Deux Garcons, or the 2 Gs, as Fisher referred to it, attracted my attention also. As I looked under its green awning at the terrace in the midday sun I saw a man and woman, like two halves of the same egg, engrossed in an intimate, quiet conversation, eye-to-eye, at a table. A grey-haired man just in front of me, carrying a portfolio with a manuscript or perhaps small prints, called out some indistinguishable name that sounded like "Vivienne," and, immediately, a woman with curly spaniel hair, wearing a black dress topped with a striped red, yellow, and black top worthy of a Matisse model, and with a vivid tomato-red purse slung over her shoulder, rose to meet him and disappeared into his bear hug and passionate kiss. It was the beginning of a French motion picture I had been dying to see, I decided. I called it *Le Retour de Monsieur Drouet*.

Later, in the market, another drama caught my interest. A man sat under a blue and white scalloped umbrella selling jars of honey of all shades of amber. He wore a soft tan fedora pulled down in front and back, a striking, honey-colored, handmade cardigan sweater, and he had a full beard and flowing hair. He looked at this moment the way I thought Paul Cezanne would look, or should look, if he were alive today.

A tall, dark, intense young man came up to his stand, asked the man something which I could not hear, and then, conscious that I was intruding into other people's scenes, I moved on—another moment in my traveling motion picture.

Soon I found myself in the dazzling flower market, where a woman in sunglasses with a brassy voice was berating someone for smelling the flowers too strongly.

And, finally, out on the Cours Mirabeau again, I came upon a woman quietly sitting with her two daughters on either side of her on a bench simply waiting or watching the stream of life pass by. Could they be the ghosts of M.F.K. Fisher and her daughters, Anne and Mary, I wondered, still present in this city they so loved?

The Cours Mirabeau is not the only interesting section in this town of about 180,000 inhabitants. There is also the Mazarin Quarter, where M.F.K. Fisher and her daughters lived on the rue Cardinale. The streets here are laid out in a grid pattern designed by Archbishop Mazarin in the 17th century and the homes are those of the old aristocracy, many transformed into new uses, such as the Darius Milhaud Music Conservatory in the old Hotel de Caumon; the Granet Museum in the old Palace of Malta, featuring paintings by Granet, Gericault Cezanne and others; and the Paul Arbaud Museum, the specialty of which is Provencal earthenware.

In the Mazarin Quarter is also found La Place des Quatres Dolphins, a graceful fountain with spouting dolphins and topped by a pine cone, from 1667, situated in a square with sturdy, handsome, tall houses flanking it. Fisher wrote that "It seems unlikely that anyone can pass by this exquisite whole without feeling reassured in some firm way." As usual, she is right.

Much of Aix-en-Provence centers on the Old Town, and the centerpiece here is the extraordinary Cathedrale St. Saveur, because one can see in it quite clearly all architectural styles from the 5th to the 17th centuries. It is like a course in architecture all in itself. The foundations are Roman, and one can even see a large basin inside the church about four feet deep built over one of the thermal springs, except it is now dry. Looking at the church, it appears to be a hodgepodge, partly Gothic, Romanesque, and Baroque on ancient Roman foundations. It is unique.

Also in Old Town is the Hotel de Ville, with the vivid flower market operating across from it. The city seemed full of students from all over the world. I thought it must be an ideal locale in which to study. There obviously is so much art, literature, and history associated with the town that I could understand why one would want to dwell here for a while, or forever, as a matter of fact.

I sampled the Aix specialty sweet called *calissons* which has been made in Aix for over three hundred years and bought some to bring back to Rudd. These are little oval-shaped candies of primarily almond paste which are baked and have a distinctive, yet delicate taste, a nice reminder of a visit to a pleasant place.

Everything one looked at in town was interesting. I looked way up at the top of one building and saw a huge relief just below the roof line depicting two figures, one representing the Rhone River and the other the Garonne, one male, the other female, joining hands in a kind of confluence, just as the two rivers meet in Provence. On another building, the portal over the front door seemed supported by two powerful Michelangelo-style Hercules.

I also saw the school attended by both Paul Cezanne and Emile Zola in Aix. I tried to visualize the two of them as schoolboys. They both contributed so much to the arts, but seem vastly different in their artistic philosophies. Zola was the cold-eyed, dispassionate scientist-naturalist, or at least he tried to be, but Cezanne, painting either Montagne Sainte-Victoire or his bowls of fruit, cast a mantle of romantic blue over everything. What did they talk about at school, I wondered?

Aix-en-Provence is surely the Athens of Provence. Once you visit it, you suddenly want to know more about Provence, a name the Romans gave it. The people there originally spoke their own Provencal language, but were forced to speak French, and indeed it is located in France and seems French, but the geography, the way the light breaks, its whole inclination seems to declare it to be something more than just French.

Perhaps that is the secret of its attraction to so many visitors. It is a restful, beautiful, bustling, variable, traditional country fair one never wants to leave.

ON SHIPBOARD

The QE2 is a home away from home for people on a world cruise. Excluding the staff and crew, the number of passengers can vary from 1200 to 1700, depending on where in the world the ship is sailing, and the nationalities represented will vary also.

On Wednesday, April 11, 2001, there were 528 persons from the United Kingdom, 327 from the United States of America, 230 from Germany, 110 from Australia, 65 from France, 62 from Japan, 41 from Canada, 10 from the Netherlands, 9 from New Zealand, 6 each from Spain, Switzerland, Belgium, and Brazil, 4 from Ireland, 3 each from Finland and Sweden, 2 each from Mauritius, Mexico, Paraguay, Austria, Bangladesh, and 1 each from Argentina, Guatemala, Italy, Malaysia, and Singapore. making a total of 1,432 passengers. One person lists the QE2 as her home. Hers is an interesting story.

Beatrice Muller, 82 years old, has been living aboard in Cabin 4068, an inside stateroom, since January 2000.

She and her husband had sailed often on the ship, but in March 1999, Robert Muller, her engineer husband, died of emphysema as they were leaving Bombay. Facing a big change in her life, she decided to just keep sailing, as she and Robert would very likely have done.

To finance it, she sold two of her three houses and figures that at $70,000 a year it is about the same as a retirement community would cost. Yet on board ship, she has superb service in her quarters, in the dining room, and in all the public rooms, plus she gets to many social, cultural, and recreational events on board ship with no worry about driving a car or braving rainy weather on the streets, and she renews her pool of acquaintances constantly.

Naturally, she also visits exotic places, meets fascinating new people and explores new cultures and revisits favorite places.

She finds the ship's staff and crew, as well as her two sons on shore, supportive of her pioneering senior retirement experiment. And she is the only passenger listed whose permanent home is the QE2, although many others have envied her.

On this voyage, we also had other interesting passengers, such as Prince and Princess Victor Romanoff, The Countess of Kingston, Baron and Baroness Donald Byrne, Michael M. Rosenberg, C.B.E,, from England, who, I am told, annually books the two most expensive penthouse suites for the World Cruise.

Less titled, but equally interesting, were a very tall reptilian couple from England, both of whom dressed in what looked like fish scales for formal occasions. Coupled with their sallow, unsmiling, hooded eyes, they always gave the impression of rearing lizards as they slid through the corridors. I saw them too often, as their habitat was in our area of the ship—pretty scary stuff.

Another interesting passenger was called Disco Dorothy because she always showed up in the Yacht Club dancing her Ruby Keeler heart out dizzily. And, although she was young at heart, Dorothy was one of those sprightly nightly ladies of indeterminate age.

Our friend, Barbara Stanwyck, was a gas too. She was a young Texas widow with an honest, open face and personality to match that made everyone like her because of her guilelessness and friendliness.

She loved denim and wore it frequently, not even causing comment from the old-line British who abhor it. Barbara was fun to be with. She was along on the trip I took to Elephanta Island in Bombay, an innocent Henry James' heroine adrift in an ancient, sophisticated culture.

We also had good friends in Harry and Evelyn Barkan from Pennsylvania. They were the computer experts on board ship and taught classes which Rudd attended. We would have drinks with them occasionally in the Chart Room and they were part of the marooned group on the pier at Vung Tau in Viet Nam, so we had all been through some sort of war experience together. Their table was not far from ours in the dining room. Evelyn and Harry were always cheerful, intelligent conversationalists, excellent company.

One of the best things about the little isle of England that is the QE2 is that you may have as much or as little of society as you wish. Nobody forces anything on you; you don't have to do a damned thing if you don't wish to. It is not an "All-right, everyone-into-the-swimming-pool" kind of ship. You can even take all your meals in solitary splendor in your cabin, if you wish, as I sometimes did when I wanted an American peanut butter sandwich for lunch and didn't wish to be stared at or characterized as "that old American man who eats like a child."

E-Mail from Verna Rudd Kenvin, Cabin no. 4127
To: Brooke, Heather, Rob and Joan
Date: Tuesday, April 10

. . . P has already left on his tour to Aix-en-Provence. Since there is a lot of walking, I decided not to go. Yesterday I went on the tour of Marseille and the charming village of Cassis, while P went to Arles and Les Baux. His tour was eight hours, mine four, so I thought it wiser to take the shorter one. Even then, I did not walk up the 200 steps to the cathedral with a very cold Mistral wind blowing.

But I did walk down to the village of Cassis. My high point there was buying and eating the most delicious croissant I have ever had. Then I had to turn back to get back to the bus on time.

The wind is strong and bitter. Today it is less, but I think I will stay on board and catch up on my diary. Only ten more days to go before we see New York. And only one more tour to go, in Lisbon. It sounds as though I will be happy to get off the ship, because I will be. Ninety days is too much, but it got us where we wanted to go, and at a price we wanted, so no real complaints.

Our stay in Naples was fine, but the trip to Capri brought cold and wind that we had not expected. As a result, I got a worse cold. But how wonderful to sip my *citron pressé* on the porch of the nicest hotel there, the Quisisana, and watch the world go by. Italy is always a delight to be in again—the people are so vital—but Venice is my preferred locale still.

An interesting part of the Capri visit was seeing Dr. Axel Munthe's home. He was not only a doctor, but also a writer who loved gardens and built an extremely lovely one with such a variety of plants. In Capri, everything seems to bloom at the same time, whereas the same plants bloom at different times in southern California.

We noticed, in the newspaper, and also Dylan told us on the phone, that Los Angeles had more rain. The temperature in Boston seems to have stayed above freezing, so we hope that bodes well for the farm . . . .

Love,

Mom/Rudd

STANDING ON THE EDGE

In the 1950s in Europe there was a popular song called in French *Avril en Portugal*. I remember we used to ice skate to it at the town rink in Gstaad, Switzerland. It was a smooth, flowing tune that one could glide nicely to, getting the most out of each forward move.

We first visited Portugal in 1988, arriving by way of Spain, and my impressions of it were very different from the romantic cast of the song. But this time in 2001, the first line in my journal for this entry reads, "April 12, 2001. Docked in Lisbon. Beautiful day. Lisbon looks extremely good—pink and white in sunlight."

Our bus took us first through Estoril, that fashionable resort favored so much by exiled royalty in the past, and then we spent some time in Cascais (pronounced CASH-kice), a little fishing village now being gentrified into a kind of California Carmel for well-heeled vacationers. I was able to walk around this colorful pink town with ease, photographing a statue of Don Pedro the First, fishmongers, shoeshine men, picturesque buildings, and glimpses of the sea nearby.

Then we traveled to Capa di Roca, the westernmost point of all Europe, complete with high cliffs, flowery meadows, a beautiful lighthouse, rocks, and the Atlantic stretching out blue and beautiful before one, as it must have done for Magellan, Vasco de Gama and other adventurers in the great days of exploration. It was exhilarating, standing on the very edge of Europe, looking out at the sea that offered the ultimate challenge to the early navigators.

We threaded our way on and over mountains and cliffs until we came to the tile-roofed village of Sintra, a town we had aimed for, but missed in 1988 because our bus broke down. Here was a Portuguese hill town to rival Erice in Sicily, Lucca in Tuscany, Les Baux in Provence, Eze-sur-Mer and St. Paul de Vence in France, among others.

Sintra is where England's Lord Byron lived for a while and on which he based "Childe Harold." Composers Richard Wagner and Richard Strauss also loved this green mountain and valley town which has its own unique micro climate.

While we were there, it was difficult to appreciate its qualities because there were many tourists in automobiles providing intense congestion, but the setting certainly was a perfect Shangri-La for a town not far from the surging sea.

Back in Lisbon, which we had explored at greater length in 1988, we drove along the extensive waterfront seeing the huge, powerful, white monument to Henry the Navigator with the sprawling palace behind it.

As we passed fort after fort, our guide, Helena, told us there were forty-four of them in all, "built to ward off the pirates. Don't you think it was an over-reaction?" We laughed and agreed.

ON SHIPBOARD

Late one afternoon I was sitting by a window, but looking in this time at the decorations put up for the Around the World Ball to be held that night in the Queen's Room.

Suddenly, a tall Englishwoman with bobbed silver hair and bangs and dressed in a black and white evening gown, addressed me: "Oh, sorry. Just checking, you know. Do you think it'll do, this frock? I don't want to embarrass anybody. What? Oh, you're American, aren't you, or Canadian? American. I love your country. Been there often.

"I'm Sibyl Buccleigh-Brown. Yes, hyphenated. I'm so glad you think this old frock will do. I always think I'm missing the mark somehow. Not the fashionable sort, you know, and everybody's always so smart looking. No, not London. Bournemouth. Oh, you know it? Really. The Lily Langtry Manor? Of course. I'm very near it. Where else have you been? Dorset, Devon, Exeter, Dawlish, Torquay. Oh, you do have exquisite taste. I adore Torquay. I'd move there in a minute.

"Well, actually during the war, we lived in a suburb of Southampton. We were one of those feeding stations. British, Americans, Australians, Poles, Italians came there. I remember on D-Day, everyone had to get rid of everything that could possibly identify them and so they shared these things with the local kids. I brought home many mementoes. I remember how pleased my mother was because, you know, things were scarce in those days.

"My stepfather was very good to me always. My mother was twenty years younger than he was. He paid for my college education and my wedding. I inherited their house.

"After I was married, my husband and I traveled to the States. We had one of those enormous tank-like fiberglass caravans. Do you know, we paid only $2400 to bring that caravan over and back, in addition to the three of us. We had a lovely time. My, but there are very wide spaces in your country. Kansas, Oklahoma, Arizona, vast.

"We were treated very well. We only had trouble once. A hotel in Nevada accused us of taking their turkish towels. Can you imagine? I showed them our cases to convince them. It turned out that they thought we were Australian. They said the Australians usually took everything. I said, "We're British. We don't do that."

"And, do you know, the hotelkeeper insisted on presenting us with several packages of towels as a gift. They're at home now, yellowing in the closet. No, the only thing I've ever taken was an ashtray from a Best Western Motel. Don't know why.

"Do you know, an odd thing about Salt Lake City— Have you ever noticed there are no signs telling one how to get out? No, none at all."

After this angular, hawk-eyed woman finished her intriguing reminiscences, she said good night and thanks and departed.

I sat for a few moments, thinking, until the orchestra drifted in and began playing Irving Berlin's "Let's Face the Music and Dance." I always love to hear music that conjures up the world of Ginger Rogers and Fred Astaire. When the musicians launched into "Change Partners," I thought this was the best of all possible worlds, unhurried and characterized by beautiful memories.

"HEARTS AT EASE UNDER AN ENGLISH HEAVEN"

"Oh, to be in England
Now that April's there"

Robert Browning

The ship docked today, April 14th, in England. It couldn't have been a drearier day. How one longed for the sunshine of Portugal and Italy. No wonder the British head south whenever they can.

Victor and Cicely Campkin came to lunch with us on the ship as we were only to be in port for a short while before crossing the Atlantic to New York.

After lunch they drove us to their home "Thatched Cottage" on Kew Lane in Old Bursledon, Hampshire, not too far from the port. We had tea there and enjoyed their hospitality, charming house and beautiful garden, as we had a year or two earlier.

Actually, we had originally met Victor and Cicely on a QE2 voyage to Australia. They were an oasis of literacy, civility, and sanity at our peculiar table of six which rivaled the Mad Hatter's Tea Party in *Alice in Wonderland.*

Their Hampshire garden has a magnolia grandiflora out front near the garage and a magnificent wistaria tree in the center of the backyard. A fragrant, white clematis vine clambers over the door and wall.

There are also two bird houses in the backyard in which a Great Tit and two small Tits reside, peering out occasionally as though they own the place and must supervise everything that takes place in the yard, even visitors from America who might giggle in infantile humor at their very names.

Victor and Cicely deposited us nicely back at the ship and we reluctantly left them to prepare for the Atlantic crossing, the last lap of our voyage.

ON SHIPBOARD

An Englishwoman popped out of an elevator on the Main Deck and explained to a friend waiting nervously for her,

"Well, here we are. I always take the lift at the wrong end of the ship from where I want to go."

"THE BRONX IS UP, THE BATTERY'S DOWN"

"One doesn't discover new lands without consenting
to lose sight of the shore for a very long time."

André Gide

After the roughest part of our trip on the Atlantic, although it really was just a routine moderate sea, we arrived in New York on April 20, 2001. No matter where you are on board ship, you can always tell when we are nearing this port because there is a kind of expectant stir that wafts through the corridors. People get out of bed earlier, voices accelerate, cameras appear draped over more shoulders than ever, there's an anticipatory rush toward the elevators.

There is always some confusion, too. Because the harbor is so vast and various, some people are not too sure what they are seeing. They confuse Brooklyn with Staten Island, Manhattan with Queens. They are not clear about what bridge the ship passes under. There is always a dash from the starboard to port side of the ship. Where is the Statue of Liberty? That is what they look for first.

For me, I go up to the highest point in the bow of the bridge that I can get to, just under the Captain's quarters. In the early morning darkness I look for the Ambrose light and then behind it the long ribbon of light that marks the south shore of Long Island and the counties of Nassau and Kings. Then, as dawn breaks, the ship makes a turn to the starboard that sends it directly under the Narrows-Verazzano Bridge connecting Staten Island to Brooklyn.

I always remember my first trip to Europe on the original *Queen Elizabeth* in 1953 at this point. My family, who had come to see us off in Manhattan, drove out along the Shore Road in Brooklyn, parked along the Narrows in Brooklyn and waved as the ship passed by, the closest the ship comes to land on the way in or out of the harbor. I still look for them there and give a wave if I see anybody today. Way back in the late 1930s we used to stand in that same place also whenever the U.S. Navy fleet came in.

On the trip into New York, the Statue of Liberty will always be on the port side, that is, the left of the ship. It is hard to discern it at first, a thin, greenish needle, much smaller and less impressive than photographs make it appear. But soon the ship swings closer to it, excitement mounts, everybody rushes to the port side, a thousand cameras click away and then downtown Manhattan and Bowling Green appear dead ahead.

As the ship sails up the Hudson to its berth, the identification game begins. What is that building? This one? The twin exclamation points of the World Trade Towers come first. Almost hidden now by newer buildings, the graceful Gothic Woolworth Building, once Manhattan's tallest (1913) plays a game of hide and seek. Then there is a plateau of lower buildings as the ship passes by Greenwich Village, Chelsea to Midtown where passengers untangle the Empire State Building from the Chrysler Building and some discover New Jersey on the other side of the ship.

By this time, the tugs are busy herding the ship into its berth. Lots of little toots and significant thrusts as the QE2 docks with a huge block of Manhattan skyscrapers directly in front of it.

Unfortunately, these days there are never many people seeing the ship in or out. Strict security has ruled out the old New York style sailings, so today one glides in or out without much human commotion on the pier. One nice touch, however: Sometimes on New York sailings, we have found a few musicians, say a trio consisting of a harpist, violinist and cellist, playing calming music while departing passengers sit and wait and go through security formalities before boarding.

But for the grand arrivals or departures, one needs to go to Kobe, Japan or Melbourne, Australia where half the town turns out, waves, sings, sends you off in the style to which you would like to become accustomed.

At any rate, once landed in New York, you are hurled into its thunderbolt world. The first problem is to get a taxi. Now they hand out numbers. My wife and I were Number 222 this time, so the wait was long.

People you knew as passengers are now standing guard over great piles of luggage. If you judge a person by choice of luggage, now is your chance.

Somehow, people become frantic, demonic, desperate in a taxi line. Occasionally, a long limousine pulls up and someone you knew slithers in and zooms away. Passengers become adept at hefting their own luggage. That lady in pearls hurls her suitcases into a trunk, shoves her husband with his cane into the backseat, and off they go into Manhattan anonymity.

Finally, Rudd and I, near the end of the line, get a taxi which takes us to the Waldorf-Astoria on Park Avenue. We collapse in our room, catching our breath and getting a brief nap before tackling New York.

———————

I should say "before New York tackles us," because that's what it does with its jazzy pace, just as Tokyo does and maybe some other huge cities. One feels swept along on some enormous surfing wave, so that balance and stability of some kind are all one can hope to attain.

On this Manhattan visit, several social things were planned—lunch at the Russian Tea Room, for instance. I had to bow out of this, leaving my wife to have lunch with our good friend, Margarete Meyers, in that exquisite Fabergé egg of a place on 57th Street.

At night, Nils Hanson, who oversees The Ziegfeld Club and all that glamor of the past, invited us to an Actors' Fund Benefit for Aids at the New Amsterdam Theatre on 42nd Street. Actors from many of the major Broadway shows presented songs and skits centering around Easter bonnets each cast had made. Among shows represented there were Reba McIntire and the *Annie Get Your Gun* cast and Dick Cavett and *The Rocky Horror Show*; plus the opening number featured 97-year old former Ziegfeld girl Doris Eaton Travis doing a high-stepping number with current Broadway dancers.

Terrific show with great dancing and energy. The audience response was overwhelming. I don't think there is a more appreciative audience than theatre people themselves. They pick up every nuance and understand the hard work that goes into making something look easy and natural.

Veteran actress Celeste Holm was in the audience. She was the original Ado Annie in *Oklahoma* back in 1943. Rudd and I shook hands with her.

The next morning we had breakfast with Nils at Peacock Alley in the Waldorf-Astoria and thanked him for that wonderful sampler of Broadway the night before.

We also took Rudd's stepmother, Ruth Trimble Livingston, to dinner one night at Neary's, an Irish restaurant. I was not too surprised to see a book cover with a signed inscription and Mary Higgins Clark's smiling face looking out at us from the wall. Mary and John had left the QE2 in Southampton because she had to fly back to do the *Today* show in New York and then fly to Los Angeles for the *L. A. Times* Bookfair at UCLA. But it was nice to know that she had included Neary's in her generous sweep also.

ROCKVILLE CENTRE, LONG ISLAND

"Home is the place where when you have to go there they have to take you in."

Robert Frost

During our stay in New York, we went out to Nassau County in Long Island for a couple of days in my hometown, Rockville Centre. We wanted to visit my cousin, Lois McCain, and some of her children and grandchildren as well.

She gave us a nice luncheon in her new home in Oceanside where we visited with her daughters, Marion and Janet Ann, and Marion and Kevin Weber's children, Mary, Kevin, and Kathryn. Janet Ann and her husband John Vaughan, along with Lois, also treated us to dinner one night at MacArthur Park in Rockville Centre. We emerged into a strong Long Island downpour of rain. People living in the Los Angeles area sometimes forget the concept of weather.

But on one of the days, I received the nicest surprise I've ever had in my life. Lois and Janet Ann loaded Rudd and me into the car and drove us back to my old neighborhood at the juncture of Windsor Avenue and Rodney Place, which runs perpendicularly from my family's Tudor-style house down to Mill River, the Amazon of my youth and across the river the town of East Rockaway, my Brazil.

Janet Ann and Lois knew that Rodney Place would be having a neighborhood yard sale on that day and that I would have a chance to see some friends whom I had known since I was five years old.

I could not believe my eyes. The years just rolled away. Of course, some changes had taken place, but other families had stayed put, and the houses hadn't changed much. There was Terry McNamara, a nurse like Janet Ann and Marion, in front of her home, and, immediately, I conjured up the images of her father, lovely mother, sister Rosemary, and brother Ward, so that everything was just as it was and within my grasp.

Across the street were longtime friends Ruth and Bob Foy in her family's, the Suydams' house. I remembered her father, mother, sister Marjorie, and brother Bruce. One or two summers in the old days when they went away on vacation, I mowed their lawn and did yardwork for them. It was such a pleasure to see them all again.

Looking from the Suydams' house to my family's home, it was just as though time had stopped. I felt if I knocked at our front door, my mother would open it and her three children, including me, would come oozing out.

I looked down the street to see if my father would come walking home from the train station in his fedora hat, the evening paper under his arm. Our house on Windsor Avenue looked better than it ever had, even though hurricanes and old age had removed forever all the tall white oak trees that used to be there.

It was an emotional homecoming for me, so perfect in that it seemed so natural. Lois and Janet Ann gave me the most beautiful gift I have ever received.

I told Lois, "Isn't it ironic? I went around the world and the thing I loved best was coming back to my childhood, my youth, my original family and friends again." And they all were there. Time and distance do not change or diminish them. Memory is the strongest and most magnificent function of the brain.

My mother lived in that house for over fifty years. It was built by my father.

That night, back at our hotel, I called Ben D'Errico, a good friend from my high school days whom I had not seen since the 1940s and Rudd called Dorothy Treni, one of my mother's close neighbors, to catch up on news. Then we went back to the Waldorf in New York, packed up our belongings, and left by train for Iowa for the next leg of the long journey back to California.

And the QE2 sailed out of New York once more with new people aboard and other ports to visit, offering the joy of discovery, comparison, and change, as voyages out always have.

Rudd at MT. Washington INN, Bretton Woods, New Hampshire

Roger at Quisisana Hotel, Capri, Italy